The Yorkshire Birdman

Also by Peter Hearn

Non-fiction:

Parachutist
Sky High Irvin
When the 'Chute Went Up (with Dolly Shepherd)
The Sky People

Fiction:

Lonely on the Wing
From the High Skies

The Yorkshire BIRDMAN

Memoirs of a Pioneer Parachutist

Harry Ward
with
Peter Hearn

ROBERT HALE · LONDON

© *Harry Ward and Peter Hearn 1990*
First published in Great Britain 1990

Robert Hale Limited
Clerkenwell House
Clerkenwell Green
London EC1R 0HT

British Library Cataloguing in Publication Data

Ward, Harry
The Yorkshire birdman: memoirs of a pioneer parachutist
1. Parachuting – Personal observations
I. Title   II. Hearn, Peter
797.5′6′0924

ISBN 0–7090–3976–X

Photoset in North Wales by
Derek Doyle & Associates, Mold, Clwyd.
Printed in Great Britain by
St Edmundsbury Press Ltd, Bury St Edmunds, Suffolk.
Bound by WBC Bookbinders Limited.

Contents

Illustrations

Preface

A couple of years ago, Group Captain Peter Hearn asked me for some information and anecdotes for his book on the history of parachuting, *The Sky People*. I was able to tell him so many stories that he eventually said, 'Harry, you should write a book of your own.' 'I could never do that,' I replied. 'Then I'll do it for you,' he said. So here it is: a combined effort.

Both Peter and I, in different eras, have spent many years jumping out of aeroplanes, and have served at different times with the Royal Air Force's Parachute Training School, teaching Britain's paratroopers how to get to work. Between us, I hope we have managed to convey something of the atmosphere of professional jumping.

At the time that I was jumping for the great air circuses of the 1930s, I didn't see it as being a particularly romantic nor exceptionally dangerous trade. It was fun, and it was a job. What I was aware of throughout my career as a parachutist was being in the company of some outstanding characters: people banded together by a love of adventure, the challenge of the skies and the roving way of life.

I dedicate this book to those aviators, fellow jumpers and airborne soldiers with whom I had the good fortune to share so many full years and so many pints of good ale.

Harry Ward
1989

1

No. 347766 Aircraftsman Ward

'What does your father do, lad?' barked the sergeant.

'Piano-maker, Sergeant,' I tried to bark back.

'Right then – carpenter-rigger for you ...' he said, and wrote something on a form.

That was the first part of my trade test. For the second part I was directed to the station workshop, where the corporal in charge told me to make a half-lap joint and watched in silence while I did so. That was it: I was a trainee carpenter-rigger in the Royal Air Force. If I had been as wise as some of the ex-Army types who were in the same intake as myself at Uxbridge, I would have slipped the corporal a ten-bob note, which would have qualified me immediately as a carpenter and reduced my two-year trade training course by half. But I was only eighteen, and still wet behind the ears.

After the trade test, I was sent for my first taste of RAF cooking. Onto a dollop of rice was poured a strangely coloured and evil-smelling mess with bits of meat floating in it.

'What is it?' I asked.

'Curry.'

I had never seen or tasted curry. For a long time after that, I thought all curry was supposed to be bright green.

Yes, my Dad was a piano-maker. I was born in London in 1903 – the year the first aeroplane flew. When I was four years old, I saw Cody's *Nulli Secundus* make its turn over St Paul's – the first airship ever to fly over London. I couldn't understand why all the traffic stopped, and what all the

grown-ups were getting so excited about. I saw other airships flying from Alexandra Palace while we were living at
Wood Green, but they never made much impression on me.

In 1910 we moved to Bradford. It was a strange new
world. I remember the gas-lighters going round in the
evenings, and the 'knockers-up' coming down the street in
the morning to wake the mill workers. At ten-to-six the
clogs would start to clatter down the cobbles and would fill
the street with noise for five minutes. When it was quiet
again, I would get up, splash some cold water on my face
and go to school.

I had grown up with a broad cockney accent, which the
Yorkshire kids thought was very swanky. I soon had it
knocked out of me, and today nobody would think of me as
anything but West Riding born and bred. Actually, I was
among the luckier ones at school. It was a time when
eleven-year-olds still worked in the mills in the mornings
and came for lessons in the afternoons. The poor little
beggars used to fall asleep at their desks.

On Saturday afternoons there were the picture shows for
a penny.* They were silent, of course, and poorly projec-
ted, but we thought they were marvellous. Almost as good
as the Sunday School outings in the horse-drawn 'brake',
with a slap-up spread at Dick Hudson's Inn on the edge of
Ilkley Moor.

Occasionally there were aerial shows at Lister Park,
where I watched the Spencer Brothers and other
aeronauts of the day make parachute descents from
balloons, sitting in a simple sling and holding on to a
trapeze bar. It would be nice to say that I was inspired
from that moment to become a parachutist, but I wasn't. I
thought it looked very dodgy. The first aeroplanes I saw
were piloted by Grahame-White and Gustav Hamel, when
they flew at Bradford in 1912 in their flimsy contraptions
of wood and fabric. No – the skies had no great appeal to
the young Harry Ward.

---

* There were twelve pennies to a shilling, twenty shillings to £1. In
those days, £1 would be about a quarter of a working man's weekly
wage, and would buy 120 pints of beer!

Art was my main interest, and I was good enough to get a place at Bradford Art School at the age of fourteen. I made some friends there, including James Hardacre, who made a pencil sketch of me that I still treasure and who, at the time of writing and at the age of eighty-seven, remains an active artist in his home at Bingley. I concentrated on figure composition and design. The undraped ladies of our life-drawing class may have influenced me in that direction, for I was becoming aware of such things. I was certainly aware of the pretty girls studying dress-design, and although with commendable stubborness they remained fully draped, I still remember with affection Lillian Deplege, Elsie Firth, Dolly Pidd ... What happened to them, I wonder?

The First World War scarcely touched me. I was a youngster, and it was all happening a long way away. We had no Zeppelins over Bradford. No Gotha raids. No wireless to bring the war into the home. Also, we were amongst the fortunate minority of families who did not have the reality of warfare brought close to us by the loss of relatives. The mills kept going; the clogs still clattered down the street at ten-to-six; and I worked my way steadily through art school.

I would like to have taken my studies further, and perhaps to have made a career in art, but by the time I had finished at the school I had five younger sisters and a brother, and I could not expect the family to support a struggling artist. I had to find a job. A close friend had joined the Royal Naval Air Service as a boy-entrant, and he was full of it. It was a marvellous life, he said. For no reason other than that, I decided to join the Forces. I didn't fancy the Army, and the pictures in the recruiting centre of the blue uniforms of the new Royal Air Force looked very smart. That was how, in 1921, I came to be at RAF Uxbridge, taking a trade test and eating curry.

RAF Uxbridge in 1921 was the main recruit depot for the service. It was an awesome place. We spent three days there to be sworn in, trade-tested and kitted out. We were issued with two uniforms, one blue and one khaki. Neither of them fitted. There were steel-studded boots and puttees cut straight instead of on the spiral and made of stiff cloth with no give in it. It was impossible to make them look neat. Nothing worse than sloppy puttees. Later we would buy Fox's puttees made for officers, and would have our breeches tailored, too. We were also issued with a swagger-stick, which we carried whenever we walked out in our blues. We were proud of our uniform. After all, we lived in it. At Uxbridge we parcelled up our civilian clothes and sent them home, and apart from short periods of leave I wouldn't wear civvies again for nearly three years.

I remember hearing the RAF March-Past being played at Uxbridge. More than anything else, that stirring tune takes me back to the Uxbridge of 1921. That and the curry ...

After our three days I was posted to RAF Manston, for training. I travelled down through Kent by the South-Eastern & Chatham Railway – 'Slow, Easy & Comfortable' we called it.

Manston was a large and busy camp, with No. 6 Flying Training School over on the Ramsgate side of the aerodrome, and the School of Technical Training (Men) close to Manston village. There was another School of Technical Training for 'boy' entrants at RAF Halton. An armoured car unit was also being formed at Manston when I arrived there. The hangars were full of just about every type of aeroplane then flying, and there was a bewildering variety of uniforms about the place – Army and Navy as well as RAF blue. One of the most striking figures was that of the bandmaster. He was not a commissioned officer, but when I first set eyes on him I thought he must be the station commander and whipped up the smartest salute I could muster. He must have been used to it, or thought that he deserved it, for instead of ticking me off he returned the salute and marched briskly on. The actual commanding officer was Wing-Commander Primrose. At that time he was as distant from me as God, and – as far as I was concerned – twice as powerful. Twenty years later I would be singing bawdy songs with him in the glider pilots' mess at Shrewton in Wiltshire!

Before getting down to our technical training, there were

three months of square-bashing to be endured. It was the hottest summer I have ever known, and the most miserable. Carrying full pack and rifle-and-bayonet, we were quick-marched and slow-marched and double-marched and wheeled and turned and rifle-drilled by the most sadistic bunch of ex-Army instructors you could ever meet. They made us rue the day we joined. A lad in the next hut to mine slit his throat after the first two weeks.

We hated the cooks almost as much as we hated the drill instructors. Cooks were drawn from the lowest trade group. If you couldn't do anything else, you became a cook. The grub was awful, and I swear the messing officer was on the fiddle. Everything was boiled, including the meat. The cauldrons that were used for boiling the main course were then used for brewing the tea. An occasional treat was a tin of 'Maconochie' herrings, left over from war stocks. Even more welcome was a boiled egg, but you had to work for one of them: only the smartest hut in the 'line' had boiled eggs for tea, and there were a dozen huts. At weekends, instead of bread there were hard-tack biscuits, packed in 1917. We had to break them with knife-handles.

Apart from a decent meal, the thing we looked forward to most was a weekly hot bath. You had to book it in advance and were lucky to get one at all during the square-bashing phase of our training. Fortunately there was a swimming-pool to keep us reasonably clean during that hot summer, although the water itself became a bit grey.

We found some small consolation in the Naval and Army Canteen – forerunner of the NAAFI. There you could get a cup of tea and a rock cake for twopence, and a pint of draught beer for the same amount. The canteen had been unofficially taken over by the armoured car types, who were mostly ex- 'Black and Tans', recently back from Ireland, where they had been putting down 'The Troubles' in ferocious style. Led by a roughneck whom they called 'Gunga Din', they would often keep the bar open beyond 9.30 in the evening in direct defiance of the orderly officer. They levied a penny a head from the trainees for the use of 'their' canteen. None of us argued. The only person to stand up to them was 'Blossom', the barmaid. But then 'Blossom' was as big as they were. When they received their new Lancia armoured cars, they drove them up to London for a night on the town and nearly started another war. We were glad when the company was posted out to Iraq. Just the spot for them, we thought. They left their mark, though. During the months after their departure, there was a noticeable increase in the number of identity parades to which local girls would come and try to pick out the man who had put them in the family way. For most of us, chance would have been a fine thing.

We had finished with basic drill instruction by then and had started our technical training. For me, that meant the endless dismantling and putting together again of every type of air-frame; splicing control cables; making sections of wings from new timber; and stitching miles of fabric with eight-to-the-inch herringbone stitches. It was still a time when aeroplanes were made of wood and wire and fabric, and air-frames were relatively simple structures. The first all-metal plane wouldn't enter RAF service until 1924, and the wooden jobs would last a while beyond that, so carpenter-rigger was a Group One trade.

We weren't completely finished with square-bashing and 'bull', for every working day at 08.30 the whole station paraded, and on Sundays there was church parade to keep our souls in good order. And we still had to keep our huts 'bulled' to the limit if we ever wanted an egg.

We didn't spend much time off camp, partly because we couldn't afford to on our daily pay of 3 shillings, and partly because there were no buses. Sometimes we would walk down to Pegwell Bay – once to see a stranded whale – and on autumn nights we would mount scrumping raids on Kentish orchards, filling pillow-cases with apples and carrying them the three miles back to camp, and usually paying for it with violent belly-ache.

I was at Manston for almost 2½ years before the happy day in October 1923 when No. 347766 Aircraftsman Ward reported for duty at RAF Northolt as a fully qualified carpenter-rigger. What a difference! After Manston, it was like a holiday camp. No more 'bull', except for special occasions; good and plentiful grub that we used to collect from the cookhouse and take back to eat in our huts; and a permanent late pass! We were a tenpenny return ride by underground from the centre of London, where for 2s. 6d. there was a three-course meal at Lyon's Corner House in Piccadilly with waiter service and an orchestra, then a seat in the gallery of the Hippodrome or the Palladium for a shilling.

Above all, at Northolt there was flying! No. 41 and No. 11 Squadrons were stationed there, with the Inland Area Communications Flight to ferry the top brass and the Whitehall wallahs about the country. Between them they had De Havilland 9-As, Bristol Fighters, Avro 504-Ks, Sopwith Snipes and BA2-Cs. Later we had a couple of Hummingbirds, which were nice little aeroplanes if you happened to be flying downwind. The commanding officer was Squadron-Leader Collishaw. He had gunned down sixty-eight Huns over the Western Front. Amongst the British aces of the First World War, only Mannock and Bishop had topped that number. When Collishaw appeared on our infrequent parades, he seemed to be lopsided with medals. It was rumoured that he had been recommended for the Victoria Cross, but because he had put up a black in some fracas in London's Savoy Hotel, they had given him another bar to his DSO instead. It was no wonder that under his influence Northolt had an operational and purposeful feel about it.

We 'erks' were given every opportunity and encouragement to fly – and by 'flying' I don't mean just sitting in the passenger seat. Our Bristol Fighters could be flown from the rear cockpit, which had stick and rudder but no instruments, and it was in the Bristol that I was quite unofficially taught to fly by a certain Flight-Lieutenant Leslie Hollinghurst who would later rise to the rank of Air Chief Marshal and become one of our most effective air commanders of the Second World War. At that time he belonged to the Air Defence Great Britain Headquarters, and his job was to locate fields that could be used as practice camps by RAF squadrons, and then to visit those squadrons when they were on exercise. He took me on many of those cross-country flights, and several of the fields that we surveyed were to become permanent RAF bases. Like many other pilots in the 1920s, Hollinghurst 'flew by Bradshaw', which meant that if he wasn't sure where we were, he would go down low and read the names of the railway stations.

We had no Gosport tube for talking to each other. A good shout might be heard above the roar of engine and slipstream, but usually when he wanted me to take the controls he would raise both hands into the air, and when he wanted them back he would wave. It was not a foolproof communications system. He had been teaching me how to side-slip the Bristol one day, then signalled me to land on a practice field at Odiham – one of those that would become, and still is, a permanent station. As I was making the approach, I thought I saw him raise a hand and, thinking that he wanted to take the controls, I let go. It wasn't until we hit the top of a telegraph pole with a thump that took the port wheel off that we both realized that neither of us was flying the aircraft. Hollinghurst grabbed the controls and landed the kite perfectly on its one remaining wheel. When we lurched to a halt, he gave me a right bawling-out. I retrieved the wheel and rounded up some bods from the practice camp to shoulder the kite up while I fixed it back on. The bomb rack had taken a bit of a bashing, but the plane was fit to be flown back to Northolt – with Hollinghurst at the controls this time. He obviously had confidence in me, however, for there came a time when he put me in the front seat ...

We had flown to North Coates, a draughty place on the south bank of the Humber estuary. It was one of those fields that Hollinghurst had selected for a practice camp (it houses air-defence missiles now) and he was visiting the resident squadron. At a party in the officers' mess that night, the squadron presented him with a scroll to commemorate the occasion, which Hollinghurst quite properly celebrated with a right skinful. We had to set off for Northolt at dawn. Clutching his scroll, he put me in the front cockpit, climbed into the rear, got the kite airborne, gave me a course to steer and went to sleep. Nice, being in charge of my own Bristol Fighter! I was really enjoying it, until over Watford the engine began to splutter. That woke him up. He signalled me to change to the rear tank, dozed off again, then woke in time to take over for the landing at Northolt. Now, in the days before runways appeared, sheep were often turned loose on airfields to crop the grass and keep it short. At Northolt they would be let out when the day's flying was done, then driven off early in the morning. On the morning we got back from North Coates, that wasn't early enough: they were still there. Perhaps his vision from the rear cockpit was restricted, or perhaps on this particular morning he couldn't see that far anyway, for the good flight-lieutenant put the Bristol down right in the middle of the flock and killed two of the sheep with the tail skid.

On another return trip to Northolt we came very close to a different sort of collision. We had flown down to Manston, where Hollinghurst was to test the new Vickers Vesper. He took me up with him, all the way to 16,000 feet, without oxygen. In the rear cockpit I was getting the full benefit of the exhaust fumes from the big radial engine. 'Holly' was sheltered from them by his windscreen and couldn't understand why I was being sick. Flying back to Northolt in the Bristol Fighter, we hit fog over the Thames Estuary, and he brought the kite right down until we were skimming the water. Suddenly, out of the murk and slap-bang in front of us loomed the shape of a huge cargo vessel. Only superb reactions and flying-skill lifted us over it. He would never have lived it down if he had collided with a *ship*!

He was a fine pilot and a great type, Hollinghurst. In the early 1940s, as one of the few senior officers who were prepared to give active encouragement to Britain's airborne forces, he was to do me a few good turns.

With Flight-Lieutenant Bob Usher, I often flew into Stag Lane in North London, where De Havilland had his workshops and where a certain Alan Cobham was making a name for himself as a pilot. He too would have a major

influence on my subsequent career in aviation. Another
flight with Usher took us to the Bristol aircraft factory at
Filton. On the way, he put the Bristol Fighter down into
the grounds of Longleat, to make a social call. While he
went over to the house, I stayed to look after the kite, and
a butler brought me a drink on a silver tray.

Famous names passed through Northolt in my time, as
they still do today. Ramsay MacDonald, leader of the
Labour Party and Prime Minister in 1923 until the
Conservatives were returned the following year, was
occasionally flown up to his home at Lossiemouth in
northern Scotland. He didn't go much on flying. He
usually flew in the longer-range Fairey 3-D, muffled up to
the eyebrows and looking thoroughly miserable. He
always seemed to have a runny nose.

The Prince of Wales (later King Edward VIII, then
Duke of Windsor) was a happier passenger, usually in the
Bristol Fighter. There was no fuss when he came, no
red-carpet treatment. We would usually sweep the dust
out of the rear cockpit and polish the brass, but no more
than that. I was still in the cockpit one day, kneeling on the
floor to get the ballast out, when the Prince climbed in. He
almost kicked me in the head. What a claim to fame that
would have been.

Some of the officers from the Air Ministry used to fly on
official visits, or just for practice. One of them was
Wing-Commander Dowding, subsequently to rise to
senior rank and to lead Fighter Command to victory in the
Battle of Britain. He was a miserable type. He never took
the 'erks' for a flight, and we had to load the passenger
cockpit with ballast instead. Whenever we saw his car
coming, we used to dive out of sight in the latrines. When
he tipped a Bristol onto its nose while taxi-ing out one day,
nobody took any notice of his shouts for help, and it was a
long time before a flight-sergeant could round up a gang
to right the machine.

Towards the end of 1925, a new unit made its appearance
at RAF Northolt: a parachute section. Parachutes? Now
there was a dodgy piece of kit! Actually we didn't know

much about them: we didn't have any. Amazing as it may seem now, the RAF had flown without parachutes right up until 1925. Even during the First World War none of the Allied air forces had been issued with chutes, even though they would have saved thousands of lives and even though the Germans used them in the later stages of the conflict. Although there had been a bit of a stink about that, as soon as fliers were no longer shooting each other out of the sky, their attitude towards the parachute quickly reverted to the traditional one of distrust and disdain.

The parachute had grown up on the fairgrounds of Europe and America. For the first hundred years of its life it had served no purpose other than aerial showmanship of a particularly sensational and often fatal nature. Parachutes had become firmly associated with loss of life rather than the saving of it. Serious aviators didn't want anything to do with them. They believed that, if something went wrong, it would be far better to stick with the aircraft and try to put it down, rather than jump out of it. Certainly I had never heard any of the pilots that I flew with regret the lack of a parachute, and when early in 1925 it was announced that the RAF was to be equipped with the Irvin manually operated chute, it was seen as a bit of a joke. 'Where are we going to put the bloody thing?' they were all complaining.

To overcome this traditional mistrust, a small team of RAF jumpers was formed to tour the flying-stations and to give demonstrations and instruction to air-crew. They were to be based at Northolt and were drawn from the Parachute Development Unit at RAF Henlow. Before moving to Henlow they had been C Flight of the Aeroplane and Armament Experimental Establishment at Martlesham Heath, where they had done a lot of the early experimental work on life-saving parachutes under Flight-Lieutenant John Potter and Sergeant Hawkins. We thought they all needed their heads examining. At Martlesham they had been known as 'The Loonies'.

2

'The Loonies'

The man who set up the parachute section at Northolt was Corporal Arthur East. Of all 'The Loonies', he and Leading Aircraftsman 'Brainy' Dobbs had gained a particular reputation in this crazy business for leaping out of perfectly sound aeroplanes. His boss was Flight-Lieutenant Soden, who had flown in the First World War and was quite a pilot. He was also something of a socialite and a popular figure on the air-race circuit of the 1920s. As a member of the Seven Light Aeroplane Club, he had his own kite, an Austin Whippet. He kept it at Northolt, where I used to service it for him. It was a beautiful little plane, and I would love to have taken it up; but there was no chance of that. My 'lessons' in the Bristol Fighter had been quite off the record, and it would be some time before I was officially licensed to fly.

Shortly after Corporal East had established the parachute section, Soden asked me if I would like to be trained as a packer. I wouldn't mind packing the things but certainly had no intention of ever using them. It would be a change. So I agreed to take on the job, and Corporal East gave me my first lessons in parachute-packing.

I was surprised what a simple thing the parachute actually was. The chute that had eventually been chosen for the RAF was the Irvin manually operated pack. A flat, circular canopy of silk was folded and stowed with its pilot-chute and rigging-lines in a fabric container. The pack was closed and the covers were held in place by the metal 'pins' of a rip-cord, which ran through a flexible housing to the handle, stowed in a pocket on the harness. In use, when the rip-cord was pulled, strong elastics whipped the covers back, and the pilot-chute sprang into the airflow, where it acted as a form of anchor to drag the canopy and then the lines from the pack as the jumper fell away. Most air-crew would use a seat-pack, harnessed to their backsides and doubling as a not very comfortable cushion. For observers and gunners and passengers, there were back-packs or clip-on chest-packs. Air-crew chutes had a canopy with a flying-diameter of twenty-four feet. For training, there was a special 'trainer-main' back-pack with a twenty-eight-foot canopy, and a harness fashioned to take a second chute on the front of the body – for emergencies.

What became known as 'the Irvin parachute' had in fact been developed by the American Floyd Smith in 1919. Leslie Irvin, who had earned the nickname 'Sky High Irvin' through his stunt jumping in California as a youngster, had been the first man to jump with the manually operated chute. That, in 1919, had been a particularly brave thing to do. Until that time, all parachutes had been operated automatically by some form of static line, which opened the pack as the jumper parted company with the aircraft or balloon. Although there was the risk of the line or the chute itself catching on part of the aircraft, this was believed to be far less dangerous than the alternative of dropping free, *then* opening the chute. That was a sure recipe for death, the experts said. Doctors, scientists and most aviators were convinced that falling freely through the air would rapidly cause unconsciousness and death through suffocation. Leslie Irvin proved them wrong, started his own business, won the first US Army contract for the manually operated Type-A chute, obtained Floyd Smith's patent rights and was now about to open a factory in Britain to make chutes for the RAF – and eventually for almost every air force in the world. One of the very few parachutists ever to make more than a few bob out of the game!

The adoption of the American parachute by the RAF had upset the British manufacturers, of course. They had only themselves to blame. For some five years Calthrop and Holt had been waging verbal war over the relative merits of their respective systems – Calthrop's static-line-operated 'Guardian Angel' and Holt's manually operated 'Autochute'.

While they were arguing, across the Atlantic the Irvin chutes had been going about the business of actually saving lives, and when this was pointed out in very strong terms by the influential editor of *The Aeroplane*, C.G. Grey, the Air Ministry had at least taken steps to evaluate and then order the American equipment.

Flight-Lieutenant Soden and Flying Officer Pierce had been sent to the States early in 1925. They were given a technical introduction to the parachute at Irvin's Buffalo factory, then a live introduction at the Air Service Technical School at Chanute Field. Neither of them enjoyed their jumping. They were fliers, with that deeply ingrained belief that a pilot's place is in the cockpit, not falling out of it. More credit to them for completing their jump training and bringing back their experience and six trainer-main parachutes to Henlow, where East and Dobbs and the rest of the professional 'Loonies' were soon flinging themselves about the sky quite happily. At the same time they were still carrying out trials on other chutes. The Italian 'Salvatore' was a great favourite, not because it was a particularly good parachute but because it came in a leather carrying-bag which made a handsome weekend case. With the Holt 'Autochute', the team was making free-fall drops from a deliberately spun aircraft. We all thought they needed their heads examining.

Their efforts in 1925 to persuade the Air Force that the parachute was a sensible and safe piece of kit met with an early setback. They had flown a Fairey Fawn down to Andover to demonstrate the chute and to train anyone daft enough to volunteer for a jump. Sergeant Wilson of No. 12 Squadron was one of the brave few. He was shown how to climb from the rear cockpit of the biplane and descend the fuselage ladder until he was on the bottom rung, where he would hang on with one hand, grasp the rip-cord ring with the other, then fall off backwards and *pull*. On the ground, it was simple. At a thousand feet it becomes a different game altogether.

Sergeant Wilson struggled into the prop-blast and slowly climbed down the ladder until he was clinging to it with nothing beneath him but fresh air. He got as far as the letting-go, then changed his mind. As he fell away, he released his grip on the rip-cord and with both hands made a frantic grab for the bottom rung as it passed his face. He missed it and tumbled away into space. He obviously couldn't find the rip-cord ring again, for he fell to his death without pulling it. It merely confirmed what most of us thought about parachuting: very dodgy.

After that, most of the training jumps were made by the 'lift-off' or 'pull-off' method, to which Soden had been subjected in the States. Instead of falling free and then operating the chute, the jumper would stand out on the wing of a Vimy biplane bomber and pull the rip-cord while he was still holding on to the rear outer strut. Whether he liked it or not, he would then be yanked bodily from the wing as the parachute streamed and caught the airflow. A bit hair-raising, but at least it ensured that the chute was open before the jumper was committed to the air.

A little excitement came our way at Northolt during the short-lived General Strike of 1926. The government used all its resources, including the armed forces, to break the unions. In the absence of the usual newspapers, it promoted its own cause by publishing the *British Gazette*. Nightly, a Vickers Vernon would fly out of Northolt carrying copies of the pamphlet to the northern cities. The papers would be rushed from the London presses out to the airfield by City types in their sports cars. They would also bring champagne, plovers' eggs and girls, and enjoy a right old picnic on the airfield. To make sure that nobody interfered with either the newspaper delivery or the picnics, we 'erks' would man machine-guns round the airfield perimeter.

As soon as the parachute section was ready, the demonstration team under Flying Officer Grace moved in to use Northolt as their base, and I was kept busy repacking their 'trainer-mains', as well as looking after the chutes of the resident squadrons. Soden often used to pop in, so I wasn't too concerned when he came in one day and stood there by the bench watching me pack one of the trainer-mains. I thought he was just checking me out. He watched in silence as I stowed the lines and then the canopy; then, when I had closed the pack and was jamming the rip-cord pins home, he suddenly said,

'Would you jump with that?'

'Of course,' I said.

I didn't hesitate. You see, I thought he was merely testing my competence as a packer, not my potential as a jumper.

'Come on then,' he said.

What a mug! Nothing had been further from my mind than volunteering for a jump, but in a round-about way that was exactly what I had done. It had been a neat trap, and I had fallen right into it. There was no way out, other than funking it altogether. I wasn't going to do that. As I was to discover much later, when a chap verbally commits himself to a parachute jump, it becomes a battle between fear and pride – or, if you like, between fear of actually doing it and fear of being thought a chicken. I wasn't going to be anyone's chicken.

So in a bit of a daze I followed Soden out of the packing-room, carrying the trainer-main. He told me that it was a demonstration for some visiting brass, and he wanted to show them that you didn't have to be an experienced jumper to make a perfectly safe descent. I didn't care who the show was for. Harry Ward was the only person I was thinking of at that moment.

Perhaps I was dreaming. Perhaps I would wake up in a cold sweat in my bunk before the dream got really bad. But I didn't wake up, and there I was in a Sidcot flying-suit, with Corporal East helping me on with the chute and checking the buckles and the rip-cord ring, and grinning wickedly. Sergeant 'Timber' Woods, the pilot of the Vimy, was grinning too. Everyone was grinning. Except me.

Word had gone round the camp. 'Harry Ward is going to do a jump ... Harry Ward is going to do a jump ...' All the 'erks' were leaving their work and coming down to the airfield to watch. 'Must be bloody barmy,' they were saying, and that was exactly what I was thinking as Corporal East installed me on the tiny platform that had been added to the lower wing of the Vimy. Bloody barmy ... I was right out on the tip, facing aft and holding on to the rear outer strut.

'Don't let go,' he grinned. 'Not till I tell you.'

There was no bloody fear of that.

He climbed into the nose-gunner's cockpit. The two Rolls Royce Eagles coughed and roared into life, and the whole kite seemed to be trying to shake itself to pieces as we taxied out across the field. It was happening. It was actually happening ... I was terrified. The grass was moving faster and faster, streaming out behind us as though it was on rollers, and the airflow was building against my back and pressing me against the strut which suddenly seemed very fragile. Then the bumping ceased and was replaced by a more gentle vibration and a swaying motion, and the ground was receding. We were airborne. That brought no comfort. Fall off before the plane got to 500 feet, and there wouldn't be time to open the chute before I hit the ground. I clung to that strut like a lover. I watched Uxbridge slowly unroll below me, then tilt as we banked off to port. Southall ... Harrow School ... over the Ruislip Road and the airfield ... Uxbridge again ... It took two circuits and twenty of the longest minutes I have ever known for the old Vimy to climb to 2,000 feet. Petrified, I was. Then we were levelling off and running in over the Ruislip Road again. I looked over my right shoulder. Corporal East seemed miles away in the snug safety of his cockpit. He was making a spiralling motion with his hand. Turn round. Oh Christ!

Still hugging the strut, I shuffled round on the little platform until I was poised on the rear edge of the wing. The air blast was full in my face now, stinging my eyes, trying to tear me loose. Clinging to the strut with one hand, I reached for the metal ring of the rip-cord with the other. East had his hand raised. Oh Christ! Don't let it fall! Don't ever let it fall!

Down it went. I took a deep breath and yanked the ring. Nothing happened. For one long second I thought that the chute wasn't going to work ... that we'd have to go down ... that I wouldn't have to jump after all. Next thing I knew I was looking up between my legs at the kite disappearing into the distance, while a huge hand was dragging me through the air by the scruff of my neck. Then I swung down beneath the chute. It was the most beautiful thing I had ever seen. It *had* worked! It *had* opened!

After the roar of the engines and the vibration of the wing and the whip of the airstream, the sudden quietness and stillness as I swung gently under the canopy were incredible. Then I heard the birds. I was drifting in over the woods that bordered the western edge of the airfield, and the air was full of birdsong, coming closer, and then the voices of the blokes running across the grass to where I was about to land ... 'Good old Harry! Good old Harry!'

Corporal East hadn't said anything about landing. Getting off was all that mattered: the rest of the descent could look after itself. So the ground just came up and hit me. It didn't hurt. But I didn't get up. I just lay there, in that lovely grass, looking up at all that sky, and laughing. I was a 'Loony'.

But I was only a one-jump 'Loony' and had no immediate desire to become a permanent one. The coming down had been great, but the going up had been absolutely terrifying and was an experience I was in no hurry to repeat. I was quite happy to bask in the admiration of the other 'erks' for a few days, then return to the job of packing parachutes, with no more thought of jumping with them. Whenever Soden came in after that, I was always very careful what I said to him.

Meanwhile, the demonstration team continued its rather thankless job of trying to convince the RAF that this parachuting business was a good idea. They didn't have much success. Flying types retained that supreme confidence in their ability to put the kite down if anything went wrong with it, and that firm belief of the aviator that fatal crashes happened only to someone else. Because they had never before had a parachute to turn to, that was the only way they *could* think, otherwise they would have had no business being up there. It was an inbred attitude, and not easy to shift.

I came across an extreme example of it when I flew over

to Stag Lane one day with Flight-Lieutenant Usher. He was visiting the De Havilland factory to discuss trials on the DH-Doormouse, in which he was soon to die during flight-tests at Northolt. While he was at the factory, I wandered across to the clubhouse of the London Flying Club. Outside the door, someone had dropped his parachute. I picked it up and dusted it off, and flipped open the cover that protected the rip-cord pins. It was the custom when a chute was packed to tie the pins with a thin break-tie of red cotton. If the tie remained unbroken, it indicated that the chute was OK for use. In this case, I found to my horror that there was no break-tie, and that the pins had been bent back round the metal cones into which they were inserted, presumably to stop them slipping out inadvertently. If that chute had been called into use, they wouldn't have slipped out at all, and the jumper would have been dead. I left a message to that effect for the owner of the chute, but I doubt that he took much notice.

It wasn't until the parachute actually began to save the lives of pilots that it started to find favour amongst them. Pilot Officer Pentland was the first to give a *real* demonstration, when he lost control of his Avro-504 and bailed out just in the nick of time to land on Hemswell golf course, near Chester, in June 1926. Two weeks later, one of Britain's most famous test pilots, Captain Schofield, leapt for his life from a spinning Vickers Wibault. Next were a couple of friends of poor Sergeant Wilson of No. 12 Squadron, Sergeant Pilots Frost and Stearnes, who collided in their Fairey Fox biplanes shortly after taking off from Andover, and parachuted to safety. Four lives saved in the space of four weeks! That did more to promote the parachute than all the talking and all the demo jumps.

Those four became the first British members of the 'Caterpillar Club' – established in America and administered by Leslie Irvin. Membership doesn't cost a thing. To join, all you have to do is save your life with a parachute. Those of us who jump deliberately, of course, do not qualify to wear that little golden caterpillar that

marks membership of this exclusive club, now many
thousands strong.

Dobbs and East made a tremendous contribution to
parachuting in Britain during the 1920s. I didn't know
Dobbs very well. He was based at Henlow, where he was
very much a law unto himself, with his own little workshop
in which to carry out the 'experiments' for which he was
notorious. They weren't all concerned with parachutes,
and they weren't all successful. Whilst at Martlesham he
had made an aquaplane which he used to test on the River
Debden until he wrote it off by crashing into the bank. His
most valuable contribution to the parachute was the
trapezoidal rip-cord handle. The original handle was a
metal ring, which was difficult to get hold of, particularly
if you were wearing gloves, as most open-cockpit fliers did.
The ring also had an annoying and potentially disastrous
habit of falling out of its semi-circular retaining-pocket.
'Brainy' Dobbs made a rectangular handle with one side
longer than the other, so that a better target was offered to
the right hand, whilst the elasticated pocket could get a
firm grip of the sloping ends. Simple, when you think of it,
but most inventions are. Dobbs never did get the credit for
that. Leslie Irvin, a frequent visitor to Henlow from his
factory at Letchworth, picked the idea up, developed it,
patented it and had it in production within a few months.

Dobbs was a good jumper, but East was even better.
Those were times, remember, when prolonged free fall
was still feared as a potential killer and when nothing was
known about the techniques of controlling the body as it
hurtled through the air. Some of the American
professional jumpers might have been getting the hang of
it, but if they were, they certainly weren't telling anyone. It
was a trade secret. So Dobbs and East had to sort it all out
by trial and error, and it was East who discovered that the
somersaulting and spinning that are the normal way for a
body to progress earthwards could be prevented, and the
body stabilized, by spreading out the arms and legs and
balancing on the airflow in a face-down position.
Furthermore, he found that the limbs could be used as
control surfaces, similar to those of an aircraft in flight. It

was a skill that few others were prepared to imitate. A long free drop required not only altitude: it needed also a deal of courage to take your hand away from the comfort of that rip-cord ring and stretch both arms out in the air, like a bird.

Yes, East was the best, and he rather liked that. When one or two of the other 'Loonies' started going for the high ones, he felt his position threatened. Perhaps it was this that killed him. It happened at RAF Biggin Hill on 9 March 1927. He had gone down there with Flying Officer Grace and Corporal Barratt to give a demo. 'Timber' Woods was flying the Vimy. To the west of the airfield at Biggin Hill, the ground drops steeply into a valley. To put on a really spectacular show, East decided to jump from 5,000 feet and to drop into this valley before he opened his chute. He missed it. His pilot-chute was out and the main canopy just beginning to stream when he hit the road that runs along the top of the slope. He died instantly, just in front of a bus.

'Brainy' Dobbs, who had recently been promoted to corporal, survived Arthur East by less than a week. One of his latest interests was 'balloon-hopping'. He was developing the techniques of taking enormous leaps into the air, harnessed to a small balloon that contained just enough hydrogen to be propelled upwards by a vigorous jump but not enough to stay there. Drifting with the breeze, the balloon would lower its passenger slowly back to earth for another hop. Dobbs was demonstrating the kit at Stag Lane, three days after the death of Corporal East. He had successfully 'hopped' across the airfield and took one final leap to clear the border of trees. He drifted down the far side onto electric power-cables, and he too died immediately.

They were a sad loss, for there was nobody else amongst the 'Loonies' either skilled enough or brave enough to continue their exploration of the strange world of free fall. It was back to hand-on-the-rip-cord and a three-second count.

For me, however, the death of Corporal East opened a door that was to lead to my future as a parachutist. I was asked to fill the vacancy on the demonstration team.

It was Flying Officer Grace who asked me. A nice little number, he said it would be. A bit of jumping and a bit of packing. Travelling round the flying-stations. See a bit of the country. How about it?

How about it? I remembered how awful it had been, standing out on that wing, clinging to the strut like grim death. But I also remembered coming down under that big silken umbrella, with the birds singing: I wouldn't mind doing that again. Perhaps I could get used to the going up. Perhaps it was just the first time that was so frightening. Things at Northolt were getting a bit routine, anyhow.

'OK, sir,' I said. So I became a full-time 'Loony'.

It was, as Flying Officer Grace had promised, a nice little number. One of the best jobs I ever had. Grace was a good boss, and I got on well with the others – Corporal Barratt, LAC Wedlake and Sergeant Pilot 'Timber' Woods. We travelled from station to station in the Vimy, four of us jammed into the open cockpits, with Flying Officer Grace's terrier dog – called 'Trousers' – inside a parachute bag in case he tried to jump overboard.

The first station I went to with the team was Netheravon. There I made my second 'lift-off'. I had been wrong to suppose that it was only the first time that was frightening. I was petrified again during that long flight to jump altitude. As I clung to that strut while we circled out over Salisbury Plain, I began to think that I had made a dreadful mistake. The jump itself was OK, but Grace could see that I wasn't happy out on that wing. 'How about trying a free fall?' he said.

Free fall? Jump, then pull the rip-cord? That's what had killed East, free fall. But I wouldn't have to stand out on that wing, and nothing could be worse than that.

So up I went for my first free fall. I flew in the comfort of the rear cockpit, and not until we were at drop height did I climb out of it and clamber down the retractable ladder. I had to get right to the bottom of it, and it was a long way down, but I was going to fall off anyway, so that didn't bother me. I hung there for a long time waiting for Corporal Barratt to wave me off. When at last he did, I shifted one hand from the ladder onto my rip-cord handle and fell away. I just seemed to be lying there on my back, on a quickening rush of air, watching the Vimy growing smaller and smaller. It was a remarkable and not uncomfortable sensation, and I quite forgot to count off the seconds as I had been briefed, until I suddenly came to my senses and whipped that rip-cord out as quick as lightning. It was, I decided, a much more pleasant way of taking to the air than being hauled off that damn wing. I was to make many more lift-off descents but would never enjoy them. It was a lonely place, that wing-tip. Actually pulling the rip-cord and being yanked into space always came as a blessed relief.

When we used to chat in the parachute section at Northolt before he was killed, Corporal East had told me how it was possible to control the body during a long free fall by spreading out the arms and legs and using them as ailerons and rudders. Sweeping the arms back to the sides, he said, would put the body into a really fast and exciting head-down dive. You needed altitude for that sort of thing, and I never had the opportunity to go high enough to try it. East and Dobbs and the more experienced few had been the only ones allowed to make long delays, and after East died, nobody seemed keen to go for the high ones. For me, even those brief free falls from the Vimy provided a fantastic sensation of freedom and flight.

East had also pioneered the basic techniques of canopy-control and landing. I had seen him hauling down on liftwebs* and lines to 'slip' the canopy in the direction of the pull and to lose height in a strong drift. The first time I tried it, it almost did for me. I was a bit too enthusiastic. I hauled in too much rigging-line and completely collapsed the chute. Fortunately I was high enough for it to re-inflate and bring me down a much wiser young parachutist. I soon got the hang of 'slipping', though. You had to be able to do it if you wanted to avoid landing in embarrassing places, for it was the only control

* The four liftwebs were an extension of the harness, running from the shoulder buckles to connect the harness to the parachute rigging lines.

we had over the plain canopies of those days. For landing, we would watch the line of drift, then if necessary cross the liftwebs to turn the body to face downwind, so that we could take the landing with a forward dive and a shoulder roll.

We stayed three weeks at Netheravon, then moved to Gosport, where I saw Charles Lindbergh fly his *Spirit of St Louis* in from Paris after his flight across the Atlantic. Next we were with a couple of auxilliary squadrons at a practice camp at Lympne, where we didn't do much trade but which I remember well because, on the flight back to Northolt, Flying Officer Grace took the Vimy down for a low-level run over a girls' camp where most of the young ladies were in various stages of undress. They waved to us with everything they had. I remember Spitalgate too, for it was there that Bonham-Carter made a lift-off. He had a gammy leg and had to sit on the platform and pull the rip-cord in that position. When he was snatched away, his foot thumped the aileron with such a bang that it gave 'Timber' Woods a few anxious moments.

There was a little more trade at Cranwell, but on the whole the flying types remained unimpressed by this parachuting lark. The few who decided to have a go were thought by the majority to be quite barmy. Although by 1927 there was a grudging acceptance that the parachute was not a bad piece of kit if you *had* to use it, to do so out of choice from a perfectly sound aeroplane was still thought to be the height of lunacy. Whenever we trooped out to give a demonstration or to put some pupils off the Vimy, there would be an audience making the usual witty comments and cheerful forecasts of doom.

Usually we would put the pupils off the wing for a lift-off. Stories have been told about chaps pulling their rip-cords for a lift-off, then, during that moment when nothing seems to be happening, changing their minds and clinging so forcibly to the strut that it was torn away with them. Nice story, but a man's shoulder sockets were more likely to give way than one of those struts.

Occasionally pupils would be allowed to free-fall. Waving them off and watching them from the cockpit of the Vimy used to frighten me more than jumping myself. We would make sure they went right to the bottom of the ladder before waving them off, so that there was no chance of their chute fouling the tail assembly if they pulled too soon. Then, as the jumper tumbled away into space and became smaller and smaller, you began to wonder if he was *ever* going to pull that rip-cord. Seconds seemed like ages, until at last there was that flicker of white against the green background of fields, and the blossoming of a canopy, and you could breathe again. I never have liked watching other people jump.

At Digby, the Vimy became unserviceable, and the tour ended. It was there that 'Timber' Woods heard that he had been awarded the Air Force Medal. 'I'd rather have been made a warrant officer,' he said, but it still called for a celebration. We then heard that the touring team was to be disestablished and that we were to become part of the permanent staff of the Parachute Development Unit at RAF Henlow. There were a lot of economy cuts at that time, and we were one of them. As it happened, we had by then visited most of the squadrons, and there were signs that the message was getting through – undoubtedly helped by the example of Flight-Lieutenant D'Arhy Greig and Flying Officer Tuttle, who had successfully bailed out of their planes and into the Caterpillar Club during 1927. In the USA, twenty-six new 'caterpillars' had been born during those first eight months of 1927.

So in September the team rejoined the Parachute Development Unit at Henlow, and I went with them. When I reported, I was shown to my bed-space by another airman. 'That used to be Arthur East's bed,' he said with a wicked grin. 'Reckon you'll be the next to go!'

I had got used to prophecies about the future of parachutists, and I wasn't too worried about sleeping in a dead man's bed, but Henlow didn't suit me. I had enjoyed touring with the team, but if I had to return to a more settled post, I would prefer to be closer to London. I was at that age when the city held certain attractions for me that were too distant from Henlow. Hendon, just out beyond Stag Lane, would be ideal. I applied for a job there and to my surprise was almost immediately posted as a rigger to No. 601 Squadron. What a grand job that turned out to be ...

601 and 600 Squadrons, equipped with Avro 504s and De Havilland 9-As, were auxiliary squadrons, which operated mainly at weekends and for longer periods at summer practice camps. That gave us regular members of the staff stacks of leisure time. I often wandered across to the other side of the camp, where Major Savage of 'sky-writing'* fame kept his SE-5s in the old hangar that Grahame-White had built in 1909. That great pioneer of flying had made Hendon the centre of aviation in Britain before the First World War. The old hangar is still standing, and although the airfield has long disappeared under a housing estate, the memories are kept alive in Hendon's impressive Royal Air Force Museum, which is built around the hangars that once housed 600 and 601 Squadrons.

I missed the close friendships of the demo team, and the thrills of parachuting. They were only partly compensated for by the 'bungee jumping' that we did in one of the hangars. With one end of a carefully measured length of elastic bungee (used as undercarriage shock-absorbers) secured to a rafter and the other end round our waist, we would leap from the cross beam, to be bounced back when only inches from the floor. I finished up in Halton Hospital with wrenched stomach muscles. They do it from bridges now. Nothing's new.

I took up a more sedate hobby when Warrant Officer Beachfield Carter from the RAF Central Band at Uxbridge came across to Hendon to start a station band. I volunteered and was given a saxophone. None of us could read music, but we made up for lack of talent with plenty of enthusiasm.

We were never at a loss for something to do on our free evenings: the West End was half-an-hour away on the underground. During the late 1920s, young people who could afford a good time were certainly having it. There

---

* Sky-writing was a form of aerial advertisement in which the name of a product – most often cigarettes – or a London show was 'written' in the sky by a smoke-trailing aeroplane.

were plenty of preachers and elder statesmen and Victorian throw-backs telling us that we shouldn't be enjoying ourselves, but we were too busy dancing to listen to them. Yes, dancing was the craze. There was Lou Praeger at the Hammersmith Palais, and Billy Cotton at some place in the Charing Cross Road, and on Saturday nights there were two bands at the Olympia to provide non-stop dancing until the early hours. You should have seen my Charleston!

The part-time fliers of the two auxiliary squadrons at Hendon were mostly city types and included many well-known 'society' figures. In fact, 601 was known as 'The Millionaires' Squadron'. Its commanding officer was Lord Edward Grosvenor, until Sir Philip Sassoon took over. The Honourable Freddie Guest commanded No. 600 Squadron, and OC Flying was the Honourable James Rodney. They were a happy bunch. They didn't do their dancing in the Hammersmith Palais, of course. At their social level, London night clubs were the place to go. Kate Meyrick's 43 Club in Gerrard Street was the most notorious of the day, and popular with the social set – which is probably why it survived for four years before the police closed it. At her trial, Kate Meyrick claimed that the purpose of the club was to provide early breakfasts. 'What time did breakfast begin?' asked the judge. '10 p.m.,' said Kate. She was sent to gaol.

The auxiliary types threw some grand parties of their own. 600 had its 'town' headquarters at Finsbury Barracks, home of the Honourable Artillery Company, and 601 had a splendid house in Notting Hill Gate. Whenever the officers had a do there, we used to go along to help out and to make sure that any spare champagne didn't go to waste.

All this didn't go to the head of Aircraftsman Ward. The present was fine, but the future looked bleak. The RAF was suffering a series of cut-backs even before Ramsay MacDonald's Labour Party returned to power in 1929. The talk in Britain was of pacifism and disarmament. It was the start of a trend that by 1932 would have the League of Nations Union and the Fellowship of

Reconciliation even calling for the abolition of the Hendon Air Day, as well as a ban on bombing and a limit on the weight of tanks – while behind the scenes Germany was thumbing its nose at the League of Nations and the Geneva Convention and quietly building a formidable military machine.

The prospects for carpenter-riggers were also suffering from the introduction of all-metal aeroplanes. The Siskin had been the first in the RAF, and that had put the writing on the wall for carpenters as long ago as my Northolt days. It wasn't just we 'erks' who were having a hard time. There were plenty of ex-flying types trying to sell vacuum cleaners for a living in the late 1920s.

No – in 1929, there seemed little future for the RAF, and no prospect of promotion for Aircraftsman Harry Ward. So Aircraftsman Harry Ward handed in his two uniforms and his studded boots and his swagger-stick, and left.

3

The Flying Busman

What to do? Like the Royal Air Force, the aviation industry was struggling against government and public apathy and had no vacancies for retired carpenter-riggers. So I became a bus-driver ...

During some of those off-duty hours at Hendon, I had learnt – unofficially – to drive a five-ton Leyland truck round the camp roads, usually without hitting anything. On the basis of this experience and on the presentation of a driver's licence that I had obtained for driving a motor-bike, I was accepted for training as a bus-driver by the London General Omnibus Company – the LGOC.

The training course was through the streets of Kensington, Vauxhall and Pimlico, known as 'the cabman's puzzle'. Our instruction was in an old open-top bus, and on fine days those of us waiting our turn at the wheel would lounge on the upper deck with our feet up, and wave to the servant girls. After three weeks of training I passed the test (which included a few terrifying spins on the skid-pan at Chiswick) and was presented with my badge of office, which was an enormous oval plate, made of enamel. It had my driver's number on it and was hung on the uniform with a leather tab. For a forty-eight-hour week I would be paid £4.6s.6d.

I was posted to the garage at Notting Hill Gate where, as a new boy, I was given a different route each day. It was tough work. When it rained, it was misery. There was no windscreen – just a rubber sheet to fasten across the body and which could never keep all the rain out. The buses had solid rubber tyres, beneath which the wet streets were treacherous. There was still a lot of horse-drawn traffic on the road, and horse manure is slippery stuff at the best of times. I've waltzed sideways down many a London street in a five-ton bus. Only once did a lamp-post get in the way – outside Wormwood Scrubs. Even when the roads were dry, those horse-droppings were a menace, for the council employed young boys to clear them from the main streets, so there were always these kids darting in and out of the traffic with their little brushes and wide pans, bending over right in front of you just as you were changing up to second gear. Then there were the steam vehicles. Get behind one of them in your open cab and you were guaranteed an eyeful of cinders. Yet perhaps the greatest hazard to health were the gallons of sweet tea, piles of bacon sandwiches, and acres of dripping toast consumed in the drivers' 'caf' at the end of each run. I have suffered from stomach-aches ever since I was a London bus-driver.

I managed to get a transfer to Harrow Weald Garage, with a more regular and pleasant route from South Harrow to Watford, through Bushey Heath. Eventually I also obtained a conductor's licence – and another enamel badge – which qualified me to drive a one-man single-deck bus with pneumatic tyres. Bliss! The route was a doddle, too: from the Red Lion at Pinner to Pinner Golf Course, where I used to announce my presence to likely customers by hammering on an old aircraft engine cylinder hanging in the clubhouse hall.

That cylinder, fortunately, was not my sole association with aeroplanes during my three years as a bus-driver, for it was during this time that I learnt to fly – officially.

A driver called Godwin from the Holloway Garage had the idea of forming a flying-club, exclusive to the LGOC. This was a bold concept, for in the early 1930s flying was mainly the preserve of those with more cash in their pockets than your average bus-driver. Club flying was something more usually associated with former RAF officers and the society set. One of the reasons why Amy Johnson was considered so remarkable was that she made her celebrated flights *despite* a working-class background. She tried very hard to disguise that Yorkshire accent but could never quite manage it, poor lass. Flying, it was thought, was not for the likes of busmen. Nevertheless, a few of us got together with Godwin, and after a series of meetings in the basement of a pub in Camden Town, we proposed to the LGOC that a flying-club be affiliated to its Sports Association and that, for a deduction of 6d. per head from everyone's weekly wage packet, we could buy an aircraft and hire an instructor. We would be able to operate from Broxbourne, the home of the Herts & Essex Flying Club in North London. LGOC agreed. Apart from anything else, it would be good publicity.

The only aircraft company that would consider providing an aeroplane for a bunch of bus-drivers was a small outfit in Croydon who made the Redwing, a useful little bi-plane with side-by-side seats and a Genet motor. That would do. But it would be some time before we could take delivery, so we formed and opened the 'Busman's Flying Club' before we actually had an aeroplane and an instructor, on the basis that we could use the facilities of the Herts & Essex until we were self-sufficient. The official opening was on 17 September 1931. It was attended by over 700 busmen. Colonel Moore-Brabazon, one-time Parliamentary Secretary to the Ministry of Transport, did the honours. The Herts & Essex put on a flying display and gave joy-rides, and Driver Harry Ward made a parachute jump.

The chute that I was to use for my first jump since my days with the RAF demo team in 1927 was of a new and unusual design. Soon after I had left the RAF, Bill Fairley, who had been a rigger with me in 601 Squadron and who had made a few jumps himself, told me about this American company that was trying to get a new chute onto the market. It was called the 'Russell Lobe'.

R.H. McClintock, the general manager of the Russell Parachute Company had brought the Lobe to Britain in 1928, and the following year had established a branch at Stoke Newington, where he took over the factory that had belonged to Calthrop. Calthrop's 'Guardian Angel', developed during the First World War but never widely adopted, had at last given up the ghost. It was static-line operated, and for life-saving chutes, manual operation had now proved itself. The Guardian Angel was a complicated beast, too. With each rigging-line having to be folded into a separate stowage, and the whole thing stowed into a metal container, it was the very devil to pack. Its main attraction during the 1920s was its frequent use at exhibitions by a very pretty girl who parachuted under the name of 'Miss June'.

The Lobe took its name from the distinctive shape of its canopy. A combination of shaped gores and internal rigging-lines gave the inflated canopy its flat-topped appearance and curved periphery, and also gave it good stability. This was its main advantage over the flat, circular canopy and more traditional 'umbrella' shape of the Irvin, which did tend to swing you about a bit. The disadvantage of the Lobe was its occasional reluctance to open. Russell had dispensed with a pilot chute and with pack elastics and had replaced them with a one-piece cover and an ejector web designed to drag the canopy into the airstream. Openings were not always as snappy as they were with the Irvin, and there was a heightened danger of rolling into the streaming canopy if the parachutist was not in a steady position when he pulled the rip-cord. A good canopy but a dodgy deployment system – that was the Russell Lobe. All that, I was to find out later. When I first jumped with it at Broxbourne, I knew little about the chute except that I was getting the loan of it for nothing.

When Bill Fairley had told me about the Russell Company, I had gone to Stoke Newington to see if there might be any jobs going. I met the general manager of the British branch, Captain Jones, who was disappointed when he learnt that I hadn't come to buy a chute, for they weren't doing much business. I told him about my RAF career and my parachuting experience, but he explained that he hadn't got anything for me at that time as they already had a demonstration jumper, John Tranum, who had come over from the States with Mr McClintock. However, Captain Jones told me to keep in touch, and when we had fixed up the opening show for the London Busman's Club, I arranged to borrow a chute from the company.

Mr Gregory, the works manager, brought the chute

over to Broxbourne, reminded me how it worked and helped me to fit it. My jumping-gear of 'plus-fours' and ordinary shoes didn't impress him, and he insisted on bandaging my ankles, which didn't fill me with confidence in the Lobe.

The drop itself was great. It was the first time I had jumped from a light aircraft – a Moth, piloted by Bill Loudel from Brooklands aerodrome. I felt a great sense of freedom. I was responsible for nobody but myself, and as we climbed into the sky I felt quite cocky about it. All those folk down there would soon be watching *me*. It's not a bad feeling.

As Bill lined up for the airfield, I climbed out of the front cockpit into the slipstream and onto the starboard wing-root, got my hand on the rip-cord ring in its unaccustomed position down low on the left-hand side and dived into all that air. I gave it a few seconds, then ripped. As the silk streamed and dragged me by the shoulders into an upright position, I looked up – and didn't like what I saw. I was used to watching the clean deployment of the Irvin canopy as it was stretched out by the drag of the pilot-chute, but this thing looked like a right bundle of washing! I watched it sort itself out into a strangely shaped canopy, and needn't have worried, for this was the Lobe's normal way of going about its business and was a sight that I would become well accustomed to. What I did like about it was its steadiness. None of that oscillation under the canopy which could belt you into the ground with a good thump if you were unlucky enough to catch it on a down-swing. I decided that stability was worth that laundry-like opening as I rode serenely down to a gentle landing in front of the crowd. It was great to be back in a parachute harness. It was particularly nice to jump in front of an appreciative audience instead of a bunch of cynical, wise-cracking flying types. Demo jumping for the public, I thought, might not be a bad thing. Perhaps next summer ...

The Herts & Essex Club was owned by a couple of ace speedway riders – brothers Roger and Buster Frogley, who rode for Wembley and Crystal Palace respectively. In fact, Broxbourne was something of a mecca for speedway riders, who were amongst the best-paid sportsmen of the time: many of them could afford their own aeroplanes. They were a grand bunch of lads, and when they knew I was a parachutist, they accepted me as being even dafter than they were.

It was at Broxbourne that I did my official flying training. Flying instruction usually cost £1 an hour, but the Frogleys agreed that I could pay for mine by giving exhibition jumps at the weekend social events which were a feature of the Herts & Essex Club. I made half-a-dozen or more such jumps but in fact needed only three hours of instruction before Bannister, the club instructor, tested me for my licence. All those hours at the controls with Hollinghurst and the other fliers at Northolt had given me a good grounding. For my test, Bannister sent me up one February evening to fly figure-of-eights in the Cirrus Moth and make a dead-stick landing. I forgot how many figure-of-eights he had asked me to do, so kept on churning them out until I realized that it was becoming awfully dark down there – so dark that they had put the car headlights on to guide me down. That licence authorized me to fly all single-engine land planes.

I and another of our flying bus-drivers spent some time at Croydon receiving instruction on the Redwing, and by the early summer we had our own kite, a new clubhouse and an instructor called Kinnear. Time for another celebration, and just in time too for the Herts & Essex Aero Club's annual flying display.

The show was opened by Amy Johnson, who flew her Gipsy Moth into Broxbourne with Jim Mollinson, self-styled 'Playboy of the Air' and soon to become Amy's husband. While he went in search of the refreshment tent, Amy said how pleased she was to be there, recalled happy times at the club, wished us every success and declared the show open. There was a fly-past by a dozen assorted light aircraft; Kinnear in a Martlet and Clarkson in a Comper Swift did aerobatics and staged a 'dog-fight'; Bannister threw toilet rolls out of the Cirrus Moth, then dived on them as they streamed, and chopped them into pieces with his prop; some of the speedway types drove their bikes through sheets of glass; and I made a couple of exhibition jumps. The first was slap into the middle of the airfield, and the second was slap into the middle of the public enclosure. I had made the mistake of not checking the wind for the second drop. It had risen and drifted me into the crowd. I was all right and didn't damage any spectators, but the chute was in danger of being cut up for souvenirs and silk scarves.

I borrowed Lobes for all those jumps at Broxbourne, so frequently, in fact, that Captain Jones thought I should either pay a fee or, better still, buy one. Gregory, however, persuaded him that my jumps were good publicity for the company. He always did have a soft spot for ex-RAF types. He had served as a civilian with the original 'Loonies' at Martlesham. He had then worked for Calthrop before moving to Russell, and he was soon to move again, to set up the GQ Parachute Company with Geoffrey Quilter. Gregory provided the technical know-how, Quilter put up the cash.

During my now frequent visits to Stoke Newington, I also met John Tranum. He was a Dane by birth but had spent most of his time in America. At first I thought he was a right cocky individual, but when Gregory told me about some of his exploits, I realized that he had quite a lot to be cocky about. He had spent several years barnstorming through California and stunting for Hollywood – flying, wing-walking and parachuting. He had parachuted from bridges; driven motor-cycles over cliffs, then parachuted clear; deliberately set his plane on fire before jumping from it; barnstormed down through Mexico and South America. Demonstrating the Lobe to military audiences in Europe must have seemed pretty tame to him.

It wasn't Tranum's fault that none of those military audiences ever bought the Lobe. Nor was it really the fault of the Lobe itself, for, apart from those occasional sticky openings, it was a good chute, and its stability during flight was impressive. The fact was that the Irvin chute was too well established and was going about the business of saving lives quite adequately. Nobody could fault it – although the Russell Company tried, of course. On 5 May 1931 Flight-Lieutenant Waghorn, whom I had known at Northolt and who became a national hero when he won the Schneider Trophy for Britain in 1929, died when he bailed out of a Hawker Horsley during a test flight at Farnborough. He had stayed at the controls long enough to allow the observer to jump out and save his life before going over the side himself. He pulled, and the canopy was deploying just as he hit the roof of one of the large hangars. 'Air Ministry parachutes are not safe under 800 feet,' declared the *Daily Sketch*, and went on to recommend the Russell Lobe by describing successful drops with dummies from as low as 125 feet. The Russell Company had done a good promotion job, but it was unfair to the Irvin chute, and to Waghorn. Had he been over clear ground and not above the high hangar when he pulled, that extra hundred feet might have been just enough. As for the dummy drops with the Lobe, they had been activated by static line from an aircraft flying straight-and-level. No comparison.

Apart from selling a few Lobes for exhibition jumping, and making small chutes for star-shells for the Royal Navy, the Russell Company couldn't get into the market and eventually folded.

Shortly after the big show at Broxbourne, Bannister asked me if I would like to join him on a trip to the West Country. He was taking the Cirrus Moth and a Fox Moth to Plymouth to sell joy-rides, and in true barnstorming tradition thought that a parachute jump or two would pull the crowds. I most certainly would like to join him! He enlisted the help of two other pilots, Easdown and Woods, who, with Bannister himself on occasion, flew for Hillman. A right character, he was! He had been a busman, too, but a more successful one than me. From driving his own bus, he had built a fleet of 300 vehicles, then established Edward Hillman's Airways Ltd, flying a scheduled service with three Puss Moths between Clacton, Romford and Ramsgate. He was later to open a cross-Channel service with a De Havilland Dragon and to base himself at Gatwick as the first airline ever to operate there. Poor Bannister was to crash and die on that cross-Channel run, but right then, in 1932, he and I were off to Plymouth. It was the time of the Dartmoor mutiny. We flew a couple of circuits round the prison on the way down. What a grim-looking place! I reckoned that I would be feeling pretty mutinous myself if I was stuck in there.

Plymouth was a flop. The 'aerodrome' was no more than a bare field out at Roborough, and apart from the local speedway riders, there were few customers. After only two jumps with my borrowed Lobe, I went back to my bus.

Shortly after Plymouth, Captain Jones asked me if I would do a couple of demonstration jumps for the Russell Company, at Reading, as John Tranum was not available. I demonstrated the Lobe to a bunch of potential customers from China and Japan. I don't think they bought any.

Tranum himself then asked if I would stand in for him at another job for which he had been booked – an exhibition jump at a garden party on the Isle of Wight. That sounded like fun, and it was. Ten quid in the hand and a day off from the bus company. Lovely scenery, too. When former Navy pilot Cathcart-Jones landed in Glen Kidston's Vega, out skipped a right load of beauties. I jumped from a Klemm monoplane piloted by another ex-Navy type, Eckersley-Maslin. I landed right outside the refreshment tent, in front of all those lovelies, but rather spoilt the effect by rolling in a cow-pat. I was wearing my best suit, too. After all, it *was* a garden party.

'It's a pleasure to have someone land in front of the spectators for a change. Tranum came down in the next field when he did the jump last year,' said Eckersley-Maslin, and that pleased me almost as much as the ten quid.

That job, more than any other, attracted me to this business of show-jumping. The admiring glances of those pretty girls; the thrill of the jump from the wing of the Klemm; swinging down under the Lobe above all those upturned faces; the applause; and, most of all, the money. What a life! But the opportunities for regular work like that were rare. Anyone could buy or hire a chute and set themselves up as an exhibition parachutist. There were quite a number of characters trying to get in on the act, and only a fortunate few got the regular jobs. One of them was Ivor Price, who in 1932 was the regular jumper for Cobham's Air Circus during its first nationwide tour. Jumping for Cobham meant jumping every day, seven days a week, and before the end of the 1932 season Ivor was needing a rest. He asked Captain Jones at the Russell factory if he knew of someone who could replace him for a week. Yes, said Captain Jones, there was a chap called Harry Ward ...

For the first time, I found myself jumping for one of the great British air circuses. During the space of one week in August, using a Lobe that belonged to the circus, I jumped twice a day at Littlehampton, Bognor, Portsmouth, Bournemouth (two days) and Weymouth. Marvellous! Particularly marvellous was the £2 I received for each jump.

It was a concentration of jumping that I had never experienced before, and at the end of the week I felt like an old hand at the game. I shared a caravan with Ivor Price's brother, Ronny, who told me how tired Ivor had become. I couldn't understand that. I couldn't imagine anyone getting tired of earning £4 a day just for jumping out of aeroplanes. At the end of the week, Ivor returned to complete the season, and I went back to the bus. It was a bit of an anti-climax after that brief taste of easy money and parachuting limelight.

I hadn't seen much of Sir Alan Cobham during my brief time with his circus, but he had obviously seen me. Early in 1933 I was invited to visit him at his office in Trafalgar House, London. He was extremely pleasant but seemed to be wound up like a coiled spring. Gave the impression of boundless energy and iron will.

He told me that for the coming summer he was splitting the show into two separate tours, both of them to run right through from mid-April to the end of October. Ivor Price would be jumping for No.2 Tour under the management of Dallas Eskell, and he wanted another parachutist for No.1 Tour, which he would be leading. He didn't want just *any* parachutist. He wanted a *good* parachutist.

'I don't want to see my parachutists landing several fields

away. I want to see them landing right in front of the enclosure so that the customers can see the agonized expression on their faces when they hit the deck,' he said. 'If you can do that, you can have the job.'

He almost made me feel that he was doing me a favour, but that didn't stop me from asking what the terms would be.

'Weekly retainer of £16, and £2 a jump. Two jumps each day,' said Cobham. 'No jump, no pay, of course.'

'Of course,' I said, and signed on the dotted line. So much money had never stared me in the face before.

I handed in my notice to the LGOC, and in March I spent my last week as a bus-driver. I was driving a route to London Bridge Station. At the terminus I told one of the inspectors that this was my last week on the buses.

'I'm joining Cobham's Air Circus, as a full-time jumper,' I said, rather proudly.

'Must be mad, giving up a regular job,' he told me.

'I'll make more in a week than I do in several months of regular driving.'

'Yes,' he said, 'if you live.'

4

Jumping for Cobham

I was still an 'erk' at RAF Northolt when Alan Cobham hit the headlines with his great trail-blazing flights to Africa and Australia in 1926. I remember seeing the front-page pictures of him landing his De Havilland DH-50 seaplane on the Thames in front of the Houses of Parliament when he returned from the Australian flight. He had been knighted by King George for that one.

I had known of him before then. He had made a name for himself as one of the best pilots in the trade whilst flying for De Havilland out of Stag Lane, to which I had been a frequent visitor during my Northolt days. It was said that Cobham could land anything anywhere. His flying career had begun in 1918. After serving as a veterinary sergeant on the Western Front, he had transferred to the Royal Flying Corps, gained his wings and flown as an instructor. After the war, like many other young fliers, he had been keen to stay in the air. For £450 he bought an Avro 504-K and barnstormed through England and Scotland, selling joy-rides at £1 a time. His Berkshire Aviation Company, however, was not a financial success. He sold it to his partner, O.P. Jones, and went to fly for Airco's Aerial Photography Department and then for the De Havilland Hire Company. In 1924 he had won the King's Cup air race in a DH-50, and that same year flew Sir Sefton Branker, the Director of Civil Aviation, to India and Burma, seeking facilities for a proposed airship service to the East. Then came his famous 1926 surveys of Imperial Airways routes to Cape Town and Australia, after which he formed Alan Cobham Aviation Ltd, one of the first aviation consultancies.

In the late 1920s and early thirties, the major figures of

aviation, such as Lindbergh and Alan Cobham himself, attracted immense publicity. Famous fliers were treated like the pop-stars of today. Amy Johnson's solo flight to Australia in 1930 really captured the headlines – particularly those of the *Daily Mail*, which did much to inflate what was a plucky but not truly outstanding piece of flying. But beyond all the publicity and the flag-waving which greeted the long-distance flights and the Schneider Trophy victories and the annual RAF Display at Hendon, the British public knew little about the reality of flying and its potential. This lack of real interest was reflected at government level. Little encouragement was given to civil aviation, and at a time when the military scene in Britain was one of curtailment rather than expansion, the Royal Air Force was going through a rough patch.

This indifference, Cobham realized, was not in the best interests of the nation, nor of Alan Cobham Aviation Ltd. If he could make the British public 'air-minded', the politicians might take note, and more support for the industry might be forthcoming. So in 1929 he toured Britain with his Municipal Aerodrome Campaign, which sought to persuade local authorities to establish their own aerodromes – and to retain his services as an adviser. 'Make the skyways Britain's highways' was his slogan. Subsequently he decided to take flying even closer to the public by encouraging major towns and cities to have their own annual 'National Aviation Day' and to celebrate it with the appearance of Cobham's Flying Circus.

Cobham was an outstanding organizer. With Dallas Eskell from Imperial Airways, he built an impressive circus, backed it with first-class administration and prepared a nationwide programme of appearances for the summer of 1932.

The primary function of the air circus of the thirties was joy-riding. For Cobham this was particularly important, because not only would it provide his main source of income, it would also be the principle means of encouraging 'air-mindedness' amongst the British public. For passenger flying he intended to supplement the usual 5 shilling flips in open-cockpit light aircraft with more sedate rides in comfortable cabin planes. He obtained a twenty-two-seat Handley Page 'Clive' and two ten-seat, high-wing 'Ferries' that were made by Airspeed Ltd to Cobham's own specifications.

An air circus, however, involved more than the bread-and-butter work of passenger flying. To attract the customers to the field and to relieve them of an entry charge of 7½d., it needed a show. It needed a bit of air devilry. It needed stunting, aerobatics, crazy-flying, wing-walking, racing – and parachuting.

This was a problem for Cobham. On the one hand he was trying to present flying as a safe activity with an assured commercial future, whilst on the other hand he had stunt pilots like Turner Hughes and Jock MacKay and Tommy Nash doing everything with aeroplanes but turn them inside out, wing-walkers like Martin Hearn climbing all over them during flight, and idiots like me jumping out of them. He was able to perform that delicate balancing act between safety and sensation by his insistence on high standards of maintenance and flying. Those standards were to produce surprisingly few errors and tragedies during the four years in which he put his circuses on the road.

In 1932 Cobham presented his National Air Day at 170 towns throughout Britain, and then took his circus on a winter tour of South Africa. Ivor Price had been the principal jumper for Cobham during the British tour, apart from the week when I had stood in for him towards the end of the season. Now I was about to become one of his principal jumpers myself ...

After signing on for the 1933 season, I looked at the itinerary and realized that it was going to be a busy summer. From mid-April to 8 October there would be two shows a day for seven days a week. The only breaks would be on the days we would cross to and from Ireland and on those occasions when the weather might wipe out the show. But it would have to be awfully bad to do that. 'No jump, no pay,' the man had said ...

The National Aviation Day No.2 Tour under Dallas

Eskell began at Southend on 14 April. No.1 Tour opened at Dagenham on the following day. Eskell had the Airspeed Ferries, and we had the big Clive, plus six assorted light aircraft and three Avros for joy-riding. The Avros belonged to Fred Holmes, who had worked as engineer for Cobham during his Berkshire Aviation Company days and was now flying for him as a sub-contractor, using his own pilots under Bill Kingwell.

The show would open with a formation fly-past by all the circus planes, led by the Clive, which was usually flown by H.C. Johnson, a former flight-lieutenant in the RAF and now Cobham's chief pilot. Then it would be down to the real business – getting the 5 shilling customers up and down as quickly as possible. Those Avro pilots certainly knew their job. Seconds wasted meant money lost. They would aim for twelve flights in an hour, and that required not only sharp flying but a slick turn-round. Taxi-ing would be kept to a minimum by positioning the passenger enclosure as close as possible to the flight line. Ground-crew would have the passengers ready and would push them in one side of the open cockpit while someone else was being helped out on the other. No seat-belts. Fumbling with straps and buckles would have wasted precious seconds. It was in; taxi; up; quick circuit of the field; down; taxi; thank you; next one, please ... until there was nobody left in the enclosure or it was too dark to see the end of the field. The Clive offered a more sedate ride, and usually a circuit of the local town – at a proportionally greater charge, of course, normally 10 shillings. For the really adventurous, £1 would buy a full aerobatic flight in one of the Avros.

That was how several million people in the 1930s were introduced to flying – clinging usually in excitement and sometimes in terror to the leather-bound rim of the open cockpit of an Avro, or peering in wonder through the windows of a noisy cabin plane at moving patterns of fields and roads and strangely tilting horizons. All a bit different from the jet-propelled lift-off from Gatwick or Manchester or Luton that introduces most people to flight these days.

While the customers were queuing for their brief venture into the sky, above their heads – and often at a level with them – the stunt fliers would be doing their stuff. Turner Hughes would be parting the grass with his tail-plane as he flew the Tiger Moth upside-down across the field. Higher in the sky, Joan Meakin would perform graceful aerobatics in her glider, staying up for almost an hour if she could find a thermal, then gradually losing altitude until she put it down soft as a seagull right in front of the crowd. Jock MacKay would do some crazy flying. There would be a mock 'dog-fight'; a race round a couple of pylons placed at the ends of the field; 'bombing' runs with bags of flour. Martin Hearn – with no harness and no parachute – would be climbing all over the wings of an Avro, then sitting on the wheel-struts as it looped-the-loop. Balloons would be burst, supposedly by pistol shots from a low-flying plane but in fact by pellets fired from an airgun by a hidden marksman on the ground. From the loud-speaker there would be a running commentary, interspersed with exhortations to join the queues for the flying thrill of a lifetime, and to check the lucky programme number, and to buy the picture postcards of the daredevil fliers. When the commentator paused for a glass of something cool, there would be the latest jazz music bouncing out of the speakers and competing with the roar of the planes. And then – the parachutist.

Few people would leave until they had seen the jump, for it was considered to be the craziest stunt of the whole show and the one most likely to end in disaster. As the object was to keep the spectators on the field spending their money for as long as possible, the parachuting was kept until the end. It wasn't, of course, as risky as all that. In fact, on some of the dodgy grounds we used, I often thought it was far safer jumping out of a kite than landing in it. But the public didn't know that. To have suggested that parachuting was not dangerous would have been bad business: make it appear too soft, and you'd have them lining up to have a go. From the earliest days of the old balloon jumpers, show-jumping has always thrived on imagined as well as actual dangers. It was a profitable image, and I wasn't going to do anything to change it.

Because parachuting was always the last item in the show, whenever there was a good crowd prepared to linger into the evening my second jump often took place when it was almost too dark for me to see the ground. The viewers could see me clearly silhouetted against the lighter sky, and if anything, it heightened the dramatic effect. On more than one occasion the ground-crew were already dismantling the screening and the tents by the time I touched down.

Most of the jumps I did for Cobham were brief, delayed drops from a thousand feet. At that sort of height, the customers could see me perched out on the wing during the run-in, and had a good view of me tumbling earthwards when I jumped. It was high enough for me to delay three or even five seconds before ripping the chute, so they would have all that time wondering if it was going to open at all. The deployment of the canopy would be clearly visible, and if it was a sticky opening, as was often the case with the Lobe, well ... that would merely add to the thrill.

Although some of the show-jumpers of the day, such as John Tranum and many of the American professionals, gained a name for themselves through delayed drops from high altitude, those were usually one-off jumps aimed at publicity rather than a live audience. For public shows, most jumpers – like me – kept to the lower heights, where the action was visible and the accuracy more assured. Also the low-altitude drops were less costly in time and fuel, a point that was not lost on Cobham.

I still didn't wear any fancy gear. Just a pair of white overalls, which I had started to wear after I had been dragged through that cow pat on the Isle of Wight and ruined a perfectly good suit. No helmet. No boots. No goggles. No reserve parachute. From the height I was jumping, there wouldn't have been time to have used a reserve. It was just on with the white overalls, buckle up the old Lobe and away we go ... another two quid in the kitty!

Those who wanted a particularly close view of the fun were encouraged to pay for the privilege by taking a flight in the Clive or one of the other passenger kites, which would fly alongside the drop plane. We called it 'The Parachute Formation Flight'. After watching me jump, the other craft would dive with me to circle the opened chute, and I would try to remember to wave to them whilst at the same time keeping an eye on the approaching ground, trying to slip towards the crowd, trying for that stand-up landing.

By the time I began jumping for Cobham, I was getting the hang of steering and slipping the chute to land pretty much where I wanted, provided the winds were not too tricky and that I was dropped off at the right spot. That didn't always happen. I always knew where I wanted to be, but some of the pilots thought they knew better. Particularly Bembridge. On the occasions on which he flew me, he would tell me to get out in the most unlikely places. I didn't fancy carrying a bundled chute over a couple of fields and through a hedge or two, and it wouldn't have pleased Cobham either, so on one occasion when Bembridge told me where and when to jump, I shook my head and waved him round again.

'If you don't bloody go out, I'll tip you out!' he yelled, but I shook my head again and sat tight, and he had to make another circuit. He was livid. It was time wasted as far as he was concerned – time when he could have been carrying paying passengers instead of crazy parachutists. Afterwards, he complained to Cobham, but the boss realized what had happened. He took me up himself next time, let me choose my own release point, watched me land within a few feet of the public enclosure, then told Bembridge that he was to fly the kite exactly as the jumper wanted it. The pilots didn't like that at all, but they never argued with Cobham.

He kept his distance from most of us, but his presence was always felt. He was onto you like a ton of bricks if anything went wrong. One mistake, and you were off the pay-roll. Turner Hughes, great flier though he was, had got the boot during that winter's tour of South Africa when he ruined the engine of the AW-16 aerobatic machine by failing to check the oil level. He was taken on again for the

British tour only because – apart from that lapse – he was a brilliant flier. Even Dallas Eskell had felt the rough edge of Sir Alan's tongue during that tour, when he positioned the spectator enclosure so that everyone was looking straight into the sun. He had forgotten that in the southern hemisphere it shone from the north during the afternoon, not the south. It was that hardness and that insistence on what Cobham called 'a tight ship' that kept the flying safe and the back-up so efficient.

Sadly, Cobham's military style of operation didn't always make for good personal relationships. Most of the flying types were former RAF officers and seemed far more conscious of rank than they had when actually serving. Although they remained pleasant and friendly enough, they gave the impression that those who actually flew aeroplanes were a cut above those who serviced them, watched them or jumped out of them. Turner Hughes was an exception. I got on well with him and was sad when he left the circus before the end of the season to take up a job as test pilot with Armstrong's. Cobham seemed to take that as a personal slight, for he never gave Turner Hughes the credit he deserved. I saw most of the great aerobatic pilots of the 1930s in action, and for my money he was the best – better than Tyson, who took his place and became a great favourite with Cobham.

An example of Sir Alan's military style was his insistence that we wear a uniform. It was a smart blue outfit, with a button-up tunic that sported Cobham Air Circus wings on the breast. I didn't like the uniform, and I liked still less having to pay £5 for it.

To keep the circus on the road, stopping only rarely for more than a day at any one place, was a tremendous feat of organization. Long before the season started, Cobham's management team would arrange the itinerary and locate the show grounds. Rarely were they established airfields: there were few of them in 1933. Usually a farmer's field would be chosen, as close as possible to the town, with good road access and preferably on an existing bus route. It had to be acceptable for flying, of course, not only to Cobham but also to the Air Ministry. That sometimes meant the felling of a tree or two to clear a decent approach. Sometimes, as we were taking off through a gap in a line of trees, I thought we should have felled a few more. They were tight, some of those fields. And apart from the Clive, there were no wheel brakes on the aircraft. In the early days of the air circuses, the farmer's reward was normally a free flight, but it wasn't long before it became necessary for money to change hands, with a bonus for damages.

Twelve weeks before the circus came to town, local publicity would be launched, and as its very own National Air Day came closer, walls and telegraph poles would be plastered with pictures of the boss in his flying-helmet urging folk to 'Fly with Alan Cobham'. There would be banners across the high street, posters in the pubs, adverts in the local newspapers. On the morning of the show, the 'arrowman' would be out on the roads even before the milkman, planting his arrow-shaped signs pointing the way 'To the Air Display' – hundreds of them, for, like many who are superb navigators themselves, Cobham had no faith in other people's ability to find their way from one place to another. The ground team travelled overnight by road and would rouse from their tents at eight to consume an enormous breakfast prepared by their own cooks, then set about the preparation of the field. Their main task would be to fence and screen the area. The six-foot screen of yellow canvas provided an ideal hoarding for advertisement, but its main purpose was to discourage free viewing – always a problem for the aerial showman. Nothing, of course, will stop small boys and sometimes the fathers of small boys from climbing trees, but apart from them, most people had to pay at the entrance if they wanted a good view of the show. To discourage the adventurous from climbing over the fences and crawling under the screens, or even cutting spy-holes in them, Cobham had some of the staff dressed as bogus policemen to patrol the boundary.

Refreshment tents, toilets, the passenger enclosure and crowd barriers would also appear, and before midday the field would be ready. Back at the previous day's base, the engineers would have been working on the aircraft since

six o'clock. After the kites had all been checked, the pilots
– fresh from a night's sleep in some nearby hotel – would
fly them off to the new field, taking the mechanics with
them. After lunch, the screening crew would settle down
for an afternoon kip, while the cashier and the
programme-sellers got ready for the customers. And so
the day's business would begin ...

There would be an afternoon and an evening show, with
the joy-rides going all the time, late into the evening if
there was a good crowd. By the time the customers were
drifting away, the arrowman would already have retrieved
his arrows. The screening gang would dismantle their
gear, pack it onto the trucks and hit the road for the next
day's site, hoping to reach it and bed down before
midnight. Cobham's road convoys were almost as
impressive as his fly-past. He himself had a caravan which
he shared with Johnson and which was towed by a
single-decker bus converted to bathroom, kitchen and
cocktail bar – into which I was never invited.

A caravan seemed to be a good idea: cheaper than
staying in hotels, and somewhere to crash out whenever
you fancied. I had liked the small folding caravan that Ivor
and Ronnie Price had shared, and had one made by Cecil
Rice of Gargrave. I towed it all over England and Scotland
that summer, and for many tours to follow.

And so the circus rolled on, day after day, right through
the spring and the summer. During April we toured the
south-east, then worked our way up through the
Midlands, back down to Kent, then East Anglia,
Yorkshire, across into North Wales and Lancashire, and
north into Scotland. After appearing at Stranraer on 29
June, we crossed to Ireland the following day to open at
Dublin on 1 July. Just the one day allowed for that.
Cobham wasn't one for wasting time. I flew over with
Tyson, in the Fox Moth.

Ireland was different. 'Down with Cobham and his Air
Spies' was the greeting daubed on the walls in County
Cork, but mostly we were well received and the shows well
attended. The parish priests had something to do with
that. Our publicity boys had recruited divine intervention.

In return for a small contribution to their personal welfare, the good priests had threatened their flocks with eternal damnation if they didn't all turn up at their very own National Air Day.

The real hazards in Ireland came not from the IRA but from the small size of some of the fields we used, and from the local 'poteen': it was a lethal brew. Although the take on the gate was usually healthy, income from joy-riding was sometimes disappointing. The Irishmen tended to prefer the pleasures of the refreshment tent to those of the flying-machine, and much of their cash went to the gypsies who followed the circus from show to show with their gambling booths and trickster stalls.

The catering was different too. We usually ate well when we were on tour, but in Ireland it was quite superb. We were catered for by Mrs Lawlors of Naas, and I ate more fresh salmon during the first two weeks of July 1933 than I have eaten since. In Dublin we stayed at the Gresham Hotel in O'Connell Street, where I chatted up the beautiful Chinese actress Anna Mae Wong. She was being escorted by three university types who, because they were not resident at the hotel and were thus unable to buy drinks, invited me to join their party and order on their behalf. I think they regretted it. At Finglas airfield near Dublin I also met Mrs Elliott-Lynne, one of the aristocratic ladies of the air and soon to become Lady Heath.

The giant Dornier seaplane, the twelve-engined DO-X, was anchored on Lough Neagh, and while we were performing at Londonderry we flew over to have a look at her. With her three-decked fuselage and fifty-yard wing-span, she was the biggest plane of the time. Too big, as it had turned out, for she never entered commercial service. Damn impressive though: the first of the 'jumbos'. We spent two days at Londonderry, where I did my jumping in pouring rain and dried my chute in the lounge of the hotel.

Finishing the Irish tour with a show at Dundalk on 16 July, we travelled to Scotland the next day and appeared at Hawick on the 18th. It was there that we learned that the Air Ministry had banned wing-walking. It wasn't damage to the wing-walker they were worried about, but damage to the aircraft. It was a great loss to the show, for Martin's performances were quite hair-raising. In addition to his antics on the Avro, he would sometimes lower a rope ladder from the door of the Clive and perform gymnastics while he was hanging on the end of it – with no safety belt or parachute. I remember him doing that stunt while the Clive was flying over Sheffield, trying to drum up business.

Martin was understandably upset that his wing-walking and aerial gymnastics were over, but he stayed with the circus as its resident 'clown'. He used to drive a car out onto the field, dressed as a groom, with a fully decked bride beside him. The car would apparently break down, and with much show he would have the bride get out and push it whilst, to hasten him from the field, one of the fliers would 'bomb' them with bags of flour. Another stunt was for an announcement to be made asking for volunteers to fly one of the kites. Martin would appear dressed as a farmer, apparently much the worse for drink. He would stagger to the plane and climb in, and it would bounce off into the air and fly tight circuits in a most erratic manner, until out of the cockpit would tumble the figure of the farmer. It was, of course, a dummy, but the spectators didn't know that. Cobham eventually had to cut that particular stunt from the show when a lady in the audience was shocked into giving birth.

After Hawick it was Carlisle, Penrith, Barrow-in-Furness, back into the Midlands ... Nuneaton, Loughborough, Great Barr, Burton-on-Trent ... I remember Burton-on-Trent. We were received by the lord mayor and his corporation and – more memorably – by the full line-up of the 'Burton Beauties', and were entertained that night at a civic ball which left me in poor form for the following day's show at Stratford-on-Avon.

Then it was Stag Lane in North London. I remember Stag Lane as well, partly because it was like coming home; partly because we spent three whole days there, and three days in one place was like a holiday; and partly because on one of my jumps I landed perilously close to the sewage tank.

But mostly the places and the days and the jumps of that 1933 tour run together in one lasting image of skies that were usually blue, crowds of faces that were usually happy. Shirtsleeves and braces. Summer frocks. Excited kids and pretty girls coming for autographs. Ice-creams. The commentary and the jazz music and the splutter of the Avros taxi-ing too and from the passenger enclosure, and the full-throttle whine as Turner Hughes pushed the Moth up into a loop. The smell of crushed grass and hot aero engines. The cool rush of air as I climbed out onto the wing of the Avro, then dived and fell. The tug on the shoulders and the bite of the buckles as the Lobe whacked open above me. The gentle ride down, slipping for the crowd, trying for the stand-up. That lovely feeling of cockiness that you just can't help when it's all over ...

I remember it all today with some nostalgia, but I cannot pretend that at the time I was conscious of what is now seen as the 'romance' of the air circus. Yes, it was a great atmosphere, but my main concern was picking up the cash, and spending it. It was the easiest job I had ever known: the hardest work I did was packing the chute.

It all ended a little too soon. It was at Weymouth, on 2 August, that Johnson nearly killed me.

The weather was fine, although rather breezy, and we had a good crowd of locals and holidaymakers. Whenever I needed to check on the winds, I used to set off one of the small hydrogen balloons that were normally flown for the 'balloon-bursting' acts. Its flight path would give me an excellent indication of drift and enable me to plot an accurate release point for my drop. On this occasion the balloon told me that I would have to jump quite a long way upwind of the field.

We had the Parachute Formation Flight up, with Johnson piloting the Clive with its load of fee-paying passengers all goggling out of the windows of the port side to watch crazy Harry Ward pitch himself into all that fresh air out there. He came in pretty close as I climbed out of the cockpit and onto the lower wing of the Avro. I watched the field slide under my feet, and when I thought it had gone far enough, I waved to the frightened faces at the windows of the Clive, and off I hopped. I gave them their few seconds of wondering if the chute was going to open, then ripped and was soon swinging happily under my silken umbrella. I had my usual upward glance to make sure it was all there, then my downward glance to check my drift. It seemed OK, and I wasn't going to have to do too much slipping, so I looked round for the Clive, to give them another wave. I heard it first, coming close, then I saw it. It was almost on top of me!

Johnson had brought the big plane right in, to make sure the passengers got their money's worth. There was no danger of his actually hitting me. He was too good for that. What he didn't appreciate was the effect of the prop-wash from two Bristol Jupiter 440 hp radial engines on a hundred square feet of fragile silk. As he roared across my line of drift, then swung away, I got the full blast. It almost turned the poor old Lobe inside out. I was at about 300 feet by then and suddenly found myself covering that distance at a fair old rate under what now looked like an untidy bundle of laundry. I wasn't frightened. Fright is a luxury that parachutists can't really afford when the chips are down. Being frightened takes a few seconds, and there aren't many of them left when you've got a problem up there. I was feeling a bit annoyed at Johnson for having blown me out of the sky like that, and I was vaguely aware of the ground coming up much too fast, but mostly I was busy tugging at the lines, trying to persuade the chute to resume its proper function of lowering me gently to earth. But I just didn't have enough of those precious seconds. There was a sudden rush of green beneath my feet, and nothing I could do about it. I heard my leg break, then everything went black.

When I woke up in Weymouth Hospital, I was looking at the sole of my right foot. The ankle had snapped and the foot had been turned completely under. I also had a dislocated hip and severe concussion. In fact, I was in a right mess.

I was in hospital for a month, wondering who was going to pay for the treatment. No 'National Health'. No insurance for parachutists. Cobham didn't offer to pay. I didn't expect he would. He was running a business, not a charity, and I was a professional and knew the risks. He was too busy to come and see me, but I wouldn't have minded a visit from Johnson, so that I could have told him exactly what I thought of his fancy flying. I had plenty of local visitors, however – some of them prettier than others. I gave one of the prettiest some cash to buy me a pair of pyjamas. She came back with a pair that were black, with a red collar: put the fear of the devil into the nurses.

When the time came for me to leave, the question of the bill was raised. I asked for it to be sent to Sir Alan Cobham, Trafalgar House, London. That, I thought, would be a good place for it to start.

'You'll never jump again,' they told me when I hobbled out of Weymouth Hospital on two sticks, towards the end of September.

'We'll bloody see about that,' I said.

Harry Ward aged 16, drawn by James Hardacre, a fellow student at Bradford Art School.

Corporal Arthur East, who taught me to parachute. This pioneer of free-fall jumping is pictured before take-off in the Vimy from which he fell to his death at Biggin Hill in 1927.

Myself with the RAF Demonstration Team, about to be pulled off the wing of the Vimy for a descent over Portsmouth in 1927.

For my exhibition at Broxbourne, marking the opening of the London Bus Drivers' Flying Club in 1931, I wore plus-fours and my bus-driver's cap! On my right, helping me to fit the Russell 'Lobe' parachute, is Mr Gregory, later to become co-founder of GQ Parachute Company with Geoffrey Quilter.

The parachute provided a useful
advertising hoarding –
particularly the 'Lobe', with its
distinctive periphery.

In the uniform of Sir Alan
Cobham's National Air Day
circus, in 1933.

Not a very elegant departure from the 'Moth', above Reading Aerodrome and a London-bound express train in 1932. I was displaying the Russell 'Lobe' for visiting Chinese.

Turner Hughes, one of the greatest aerobatic pilots of the time, flew for Cobham in 1932 and 1933.

Turner Hughes doing his stuff in an inverted Tiger Moth at London's Stag Lane aerodrome in 1933.

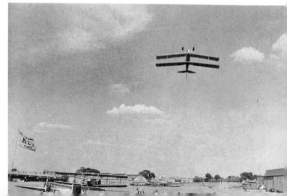

Kitting up for another jump: no boots; no helmet; no goggles; no reserve parachute . . .

In strong surface winds, the 'Lobe' took a bit of handling.

Andrews, myself and the four-in-hand alongside the 'Spider' at Sarghoda during our 1934 tour of India with Dalton's Air Display.

There was no lack of people eager for a joy-ride in the Argosy during 1934, the peak of air circus popularity.

John Tranum was the greatest of my friendly rivals in the jumping game, before his tragic death in 1955.

John Tranum and myself signing autographs at Herne Bay, back in 1933.

Ivor Price jumped for Cobham for three seasons before his untimely death in 1935. Here he makes a 'pull-off' from the wing of the 'Clive'.

'Bogie' Gray – one of the many fine circus pilots who flew the Avros from which I jumped.

5

The British Hospitals Air Pageant

One small consolation as I hobbled out of Weymouth Hospital was that I had been luckier than some of the other lads on the parachuting circuit during that summer of 1933.

'Windy' Evans had been the parachute-packer for No. 600 Squadron when I was at Hendon. He had left the RAF some time after me and had become a full-time parachutist with another of the air circuses that were touring Britain in 1933. Like any true professional jumper, he never cancelled a drop because of a bit of wind. At Harrogate, that bit of wind killed him. To counter a strong drift, he had as usual slipped his canopy. On this occasion he overdid it. The chute collapsed and streamed, and before he had time to sort it out, he plummeted straight in.

A jumper called O'Hara was also killed by the wind, which whipped him in for a hard backwards landing and broke his neck. My old friend Bill Fairley, who had left the RAF to work as demonstration jumper for the GQ Parachute Company, suffered a crush-fracture of the spine while giving a show at Southend, and that put an end to his career as a parachutist. Yes … I was lucky.

I was particularly lucky to find a good osteopath. I was in a pub in Hampstead, shortly after leaving hospital and still carrying a good limp around with me. 'I know just the chap for you,' someone said, 'my flat-mate. He's an osteopath, works in Baker Street.'

I made an appointment and hobbled off to Baker Street. After six sessions of what seemed like all-in wrestling, I was no longer limping, and I have been as right as rain ever since.

So, early in 1934, with two good legs and no qualms about jumping again, I started to look for another parachuting job for that coming season. I didn't particularly want to go back to Cobham. There was still that little matter of the hospital bill. In any case, he was only putting one tour on the road for 1934, and he would probably want Ivor Price for that, for Ivor was a nice, steady chap, not an awkward little cuss like me. Much as I regretted the death of poor 'Windy' Evans, it had perhaps created a vacancy for a full-time jumper. I knew that his place had been taken by Benno de Greeuw for the rest of the 1933 season, but Benno was an occasional jumper, not an experienced pro, and I thought there might be a job going. The outfit that 'Windy' Evans had been jumping for was called 'The British Hospitals Air Pageant' ...

When Sir Alan Cobham had returned to Britain early in 1933 after taking his circus to South Africa for the winter season, he had been very miffed to find that his company secretary, Barker, had left him. Not only had he left him: he had joined forces with Jimmy King of the London printing firm Galbraith & King to set up in opposition to the National Air Day. They had cleverly called this new air circus 'The British Hospitals Air Pageant', on the basis that it operated as a charity by passing a percentage of its profit to local hospitals – which indeed it did, although that percentage was usually small and mostly undisclosed. 'Hospitals' had enjoyed a successful 1933 season in competition with Cobham's two tours. Public interest in flying was at its height and was sufficient to sustain all three air circuses that toured the British Isles that summer.

In a November editorial for *The Aeroplane*, C.J. Grey had taken a dig at Barker and King for 'exploiting the gullibility of the charitably minded'. As it wasn't likely that many of the 'gullibly minded' read *The Aeroplane*, there was no real reason why they shouldn't be queuing up again for their joy-rides with the British Hospitals Air Pageant during 1934. I went to see Captain Jones, who put me in touch with Jimmy King, in whose London office I was very soon seated. Yes, he said, they were looking for another parachutist, but were my legs up to it? I assured him that they were as good as new. He offered a weekly retainer of £12.10s., and £2 a jump. The retainer was less than Cobham had paid, but I didn't argue. I was just glad of the chance to get back into the air again and earn such easy money.

'No jump, no pay, of course,' said Jimmy King as I prepared to sign on.

'Of course,' I said.

With 180 towns stretching out before us, I joined the circus in April. I immediately became aware of an atmosphere that was very different from that of the Cobham circus. So much more relaxed! So much more friendly towards a mere jumper and ex-aircraftsman! Whereas Cobham's programme had read like something out of the 'civil list', with an emphasis on rank, previous military status didn't feature at all amongst the Hospitals crew. This had much to do with the genial nature of Jimmy King himself, who accompanied the tour as manager and was very much one of the lads. And what a grand bunch of lads they were! During my time with the outfit there was 'Jock' Bonar, 'Stainless' Steel, 'Get There' Kennedy, Earl B. Fielden, 'Jerry' Chambers, 'Dotty' Doig, 'Bats' Bullmore, Andy Anderson, 'Tubby' Hearn, Tommy Nash, 'Foxy' Reynolds, who flew the Fox Moth, 'Bogey' Grey and 'Canadian' Carleton-Ross. The great C.W.A. Scott and the Honourable Mrs Victor Bruce would sometimes fly for us, and later there would be Pauline Gower and Owen Cathcart-Jones and Tom Campbell-Black. Great fliers! Great people! I am not suggesting that as pilots and people they were any better than Cobham's fliers. They were all from the same stable, after all. It was just that under Jimmy King's benign influence they were allowed to be themselves. Rank didn't matter: skill in the air was the only status symbol.

Jimmy King's partner, Barker, joined us only occasionally. He was probably too busy somewhere ripping someone off, for he was a right crafty type where finance was concerned – as I was later to find out.

In practical terms, the Hospitals circus operated on lines similar to Cobham's – understandably, as Barker had learnt the ropes from Sir Alan during the first tour of the National Aviation Day in 1932. There was the same advance publicity; the same meticulous back-up organization; the same daily move to another town; the same crowds; the same fly-past and stunting and joy-riding; and the same climax to each show – the parachute jump. Only in detail were there differences.

In addition to the same small fleet of Avros for joy-riding, we had a bus even bigger than Cobham's Clive. It was a three-engined Armstrong Whitworth Argosy, hired from Imperial Airways and usually flown by Earl B. Fielden, a former Imperial pilot and a fellow Yorkshireman, who was to feature prominently in a later chapter of my parachuting life. Most of the stunt flying was done by Jock Bonar in a Blackburn Lincock.

On the ground, the organization was modelled on Cobham's, except that our ladies' toilets were far more grand! Instead of the usual canvas-screen jobs, we had a splendid mobile loo made by Elsan, with cubicles, steps and a female attendant. Very posh. We were proud of our public-address system, too. It was provided by Rex Records in return for constant playing of their current hit music. I had a fine collection of their records by the end of the tour.

Our announcer was Roy Arthur, a professional actor 'resting' for the summer months. I don't know how much 'rest' he got during a tour with an air circus, but it must certainly have been a change for him. Rex had a superb voice and was a great one for plugging our postcards. All of us had our portraits mounted on postcards to sell to the customers, with the idea that they would then get us to autograph them. Whenever one of us put in an appearance or landed after our part in the show, Roy's fine voice would boom out over the loudspeakers, 'Come on girls – get his autograph! Who knows what romance might spring from a sixpenny postcard!' If a romance or two did spring from a sixpenny postcard, they rarely lasted more than a night. We were gone the next day. Ah, the public thought we were a very dashing lot! Some of us were, of course ...

The booking clerk was 'Scotty' Talbot. He had been a flight-lieutenant in the RAF in India during the 1920s but had been invalided out. He was a charming man but with a great weakness for whisky. He was a good type to have in the team when we visited some of the Scottish distilleries, but his career with the circus came to an end when he was found one day crouching in a corner of the booking tent, frothing at the mouth and barking at all the other dogs he thought he could see.

To keep the customers entertained between the two shows and whenever there might be a lull in the flying, we had a team of professional circus clowns, the three Austin Brothers. They lived in their own caravan, towed by a lorry in which they carried their props. When they had a puncture, they stuffed the tyre with straw and drove for miles on it. An old circus custom, apparently. Earl Fielden had a caravan too, and I still had my own, now towed behind a Chrysler I paid £8 for.

I was still jumping with a Russell Lobe – with 'CO-OP TEA' written in large silk letters round the periphery. Advertising was an important source of revenue. The screening round the fields was plastered with it, and our former Canadian ice-hockey player Carleton-Ross used to tow advertising banners round the local skies behind an Avro 504.

Most of my jumps were from the Avro. Apart from a new engine and removal of the landing-skid ('toothpick', we erks used to call it at Manston), it was the same kite many pilots had been trained on in the later years of the First World War. I was usually flown by 'Bats' Bullmore or 'Tubby' Hearn, and never had any problems with them: they were good fliers, and good friends.

I had no worries about jumping again after my accident at Weymouth. That had been Johnson's fault, not mine, so I had suffered no loss of confidence, and the legs were fine. It was just good to be back earning money the easiest way I knew. It needed only a few jumps to get the feel of the chute again and to regain that precise judgement of height and speed and direction that makes for good landings, in exactly the right place. Falling out of aeroplanes can become quite routine when you're doing it twice a day, every day. Sometimes, if the crowds were large enough, Jimmy King would ask me to do an extra jump. At other times, if the weather was really foul, there would be no jump at all. Those occasions were rare. If the aeroplanes could fly, I could jump.

I remember one occasion, at Northampton, when the surface wind was gusting up to 30 mph. A steady wind is not too bad, even at that speed. It's those sudden gusts that can catch you and slam you down like a sack of spuds, even with a steady chute like the Lobe. I didn't fancy jumping in those conditions but was loth to forgo the £2 jump money. On the upwind edge of the field there was a thick belt of trees. Although they were 500 yards away from the crowd, I thought that if I could land in their lee, the spectators would get some sort of show and I would get my two quid.

So up I went, while Roy Arthur gave the customers a real sob-story about how I was risking life and limb by jumping in such conditions, purely for their entertainment. I picked my release point with care and lobbed out at a thousand feet. When I had opened, I looked down. I had never seen the ground moving so fast! I was whistling across the sky, going at those trees like an express train. Too low and I would crash straight into them. Too high and I would be swept out of their shelter on the far side. With a touch of slipping, I got it just right. I skimmed over the uppermost branches, dropped into that narrow band of calmer air and touched down softly enough, while across the field the spectators were holding on to their hats and cheering loudly. They really did believe that I had done it just for them! It was a dodge that I was to use on several subsequent occasions when winds were high and shelter was available.

But the jumps and the season were mostly routine. Jump; pack; jump again; pack once more in failing light; time for a drink or two and perhaps a game of poker;

spending those pound notes almost as quickly as they came; move on to another town, another field, another crowd; jump; pack; jump ... Seas of faces, coming and going like waves, perhaps a pretty one standing out and remembered for a day or two. Kids with stubby pencils. 'Can I have your autograph, mister?' Smell of grass and aero engines. Jump; pack; jump ...

Little happened during that summer of 1934 to disrupt the pattern as we made our way slowly round Britain, ticking off those 180 towns. We kept free of serious accident ourselves but at the end of June had a sad reminder of the hazardous nature of circus flying. Jock MacKay was working for Cobham again that summer. One of Jock's tricks was to run out from the crowd dressed as a yokel and clamber unsurely into the cockpit of an Avro, pursued by cries of 'Stop that man!' from the loudspeakers. Before anybody could prevent him, he would bounce the Avro into the air, then give a display of crazy-flying as though it really was a drunken yokel at the controls. He would crown the performance by climbing out of the cockpit onto the wing-root, apparently leaving the aircraft to look after itself, but in fact holding it steady with a length of elastic attached to the control column. During a show at Farnborough he got the elastic and his trouser-leg and the control column and the throttle all tangled up and ploughed straight in. We all knew Jock and his wonderful sense of humour, and he was a great loss to the world of the flying circuses.

The crazy-flying and the stunting went on as before. In fact, we were always looking for new tricks, new ways to thrill the crowds. By 1934, many of the customers must have been coming not to their first air show but to their second or even third, and they would be looking for something different. As in any other form of show business, we were always seeking novelty. I managed to add some to our parachuting act when we took on another jumper.

Bill Hire was in the sales and advertising business, and he was good at it: handsome, plausible and a smooth talker. He was a salesman for Ambrose Corsets when I met him. That was at Stoke Newington, where he was living in the same private hotel as my old friend Captain Jones. He was still trying to flog the Lobe and, recognizing Bill as the sort of chap who is game for anything, thought he might be able to sell him one. With this in mind, he brought him to one of our shows, where he introduced Bill to Jimmy King. Bill was keen to jump, and Jimmy offered to take him on for £2 a jump but no retainer. Jimmy also recognized the natural flair of a salesman and suggested that Bill might be able to help with the forward advertising. That sounded as though it might be more fun than selling corsets, so Bill Hire joined the circus. He was handed over to me to be trained as a parachutist.

I didn't mess about with a lot of fancy ground training. There's only one way to find out if a man is going to make a parachutist, and that is to take him up to 2,000 feet and push him out. Bill, like most people, was terrified. That's always a healthy sign. It's the trainee who says he isn't at all scared about leaping into space for the first time that you have to worry about. He's the one who needs the brain mechanic, not the chap who goes a bit pale when you help him on with his chute and remind him where the rip-cord handle is, and who is clumsy and white-knuckled with fear as he struggles out of the cockpit into that uninviting blast of cold air for the first time. So Bill Hire went through the fear barrier like any normal person – and came out the other side grinning.

As he became more proficient, I discovered that what Bill Hire liked most about jumping was the applause of the crowd and the admiring glances of the prettier ones amongst them. A ladies' man was Bill. Being a dare-devil parachutist helped no end in that particular role. He would eventually marry into a rich brewing family, but a little thing like that never stopped Bill Hire chasing skirt.

Towards the end of the season, we began doing double jumps. Jimmy King billed it as a parachute race. Over the loudspeakers would boom Roy Arthur's voice: 'And now, ladies and gentlemen, a sensational race to the ground by our two parachutists, Bill Hire and Harry Ward ... a race from a thousand feet all the way to the ground for a purse of £50 ...'

From two separate Avros flying as a close pair, Bill and I would launch ourselves simultaneously into the 'race'. Not yet as wise as me, Bill might delay his pull a second beyond mine, to open lower and so gain a lead under the canopy. He hadn't my experience in slipping a Lobe into a rapid descent, however, so we usually made a close finish of it. Had that £50 purse been anything but a figment of Jimmy Kings imagination, we would both have been opening our chutes a lot closer to the daisies and making a real race of it. I think I would have won and that Bill Hire would have killed himself, so it was just as well there wasn't a prize.

Yes, it was a good season, with no major problems, and spent in the most wonderful company. When the end of a tour was in sight, you would get that sense of relief and that delightful anticipation of having nothing to do, mixed with the nagging concern that you might have nothing to do for much too long. Being out of a job was no joke in the Britain of 1934. We rarely appeared in the areas that were the worst hit by the Depression, for obvious reasons: you wouldn't be selling many joy-rides in Jarrow. But I remember driving through Workington on my way from one show to another that summer and finding it like a ghost town. Just a few men standing in the streets, not moving, as though moving might raise an appetite they couldn't feed. While we were in Cumbria, I was invited to go down a coal mine. When the colliers at the coal face heard that I was a professional parachutist, they told me I was crazy. I knew where I would rather be – hanging under a piece of silk high above the ground rather than toiling a mile below it. I wasn't crazy. I was one of the lucky ones. I knew it, and as the end of the season approached, I found myself saving a bit more cash instead of spending it like water.

It was at that stage of my first tour with the British Hospitals Air Pageant that we had a visitor: a pilot called Andrews.

'How do you fancy a trip to India?' he said.

6

Chee-chee Girls and Burra-pegs

The British Hospitals Air Pageant was at Rye when Andrews came recruiting for the India trip.

'India?'

'Yes. Captain Dalton's taking another circus out there this winter, and he's looking for a jumper,' said Andrews. 'Tranum did it last year, but he doesn't want to go this time. He's planning to do a high-altitude jump in '35. It's only going to be a small outfit. I'll be flying the Fokker for joy-rides, and we'll probably use it for the jumps. Dalton and a chap called Sullivan will be flying the Moths, and Ginger Jones has said that he'll come as engineer. How about it?'

India? Why not? It sounded like fun. Ginger Jones was one of our engineers with the Hospitals circus, and I couldn't wish for a better drinking companion. It would also be a good opportunity to make some cash during the winter, and thus relieve me of the unaccustomed strain of having to put something aside from my present earnings.

'What are the terms?' I asked Andrews, trying not to sound too enthusiastic. Enthusiasm might have pushed the price down.

'You'll have to discuss that with Captain Dalton,' he told me. 'I'm only the pilot.'

'OK,' I said.

So I went to see Captain Dalton in his office in Piccadilly, where he ran a firm called Furlough Cars, which hired out vehicles to officers and other types returning from the Far East on furlough. Hence his close connection with India. He told me about the proposed tour and of places that I had never heard of but which sounded very exotic, then we got down to the important business of how much he was going to pay me.

'£2 a jump, and your passage both ways.'

'No retainer?'

'No, but you'll have a chance to make extra cash by training some of the young Indian nobs to jump,' he assured me.

'OK.'

'No jump, no pay, of course.'

'Of course,' I said.

I finished the British Hospitals Air Pageant tour without incident, and in October found myself boarding the P&O liner *Strathaird* at Tilbury docks. I was given a fond farewell by several friends. Some farewell! I was put to bed by a cabin steward and didn't surface until Tangier.

I had another drink or two at Marseilles, in a place called 'The Newcastle Arms', run by a Geordie woman who had married a Frenchman. It was a right dive, full of seamen, prostitutes and pimps. I made my number with the lady-of-the-house, who welcomed my northern accent and made sure I wasn't ripped off by her regular clients. After one particularly happy evening at the Newcastle Arms, I made my way back to the dock, managed to negotiate a gangway and yards of corridor and crashed out in what I thought was my cabin. I was woken by a mystified steward. Not only was I in the wrong cabin: I was on the wrong ship. I had boarded the *Strathaird*'s identical sister ship, the *Strathnever*, which had stopped over in Marseilles on its way back to Britain and had come very close to taking me with it.

Andrews joined the *Strathaird* at Marseilles, as did others who didn't fancy the sea trip across the Bay of Biscay. He was a pleasant chap and a brilliant pilot but was very unassuming and not much of a drinker. Ginger Jones was flying out to India, so I didn't have his company, but on a P&O liner in the thirties it didn't take long to find a few drinking companions. I became acquainted with some tea-planters who were returning to Ceylon following a spot of home leave.

After a leisurely trip across the Mediterranean, we docked at Port Said. I had never known such heat. It was time, I thought, to try on my pith helmet. It was a magnificent beast, a real fore-and-after, that would surely strike fear into the fiercest of tigers. It had cost me a fiver in Dunne's in Bradford. Silk lining, ventilators – the lot! When I went up on deck and proudly presented myself and my helmet to the planters, they stared in astonishment. 'Where on earth are you going? Darkest Africa?' one said. 'If you go ashore at Bombay wearing that thing, they'll stone you!'

Presumably to protect me from stones, he whipped the helmet from my head and sent it skimming over the rail. We watched if float away amongst the bum-boats, like a small barge. Then they took me ashore and directed me to Simon Artz, the Selfridges of the East, where I paid 5 shillings for a more acceptable 'Bombay bowler'. We went ashore again at Aden, where I had a drink or two with some of the RAF bods stationed there.

There was no shortage of female company on a sea trip to India in those days. There was a whole bevy of good-lookers on their way East either to rejoin their husbands after summer 'at home' or to look for one. The latter were known as 'the fishing fleet'. If they hadn't hooked a husband before the next hot season, they would travel back to Britain as 'returned empties'. I had somehow imagined that the upper set was able to resist those temptations to which we mere mortals were only too happy to succumb. Not a bit of it. It was like a game of 'musical cabins' on board the *Strathaird*, India-bound in 1934.

It needed quite a few cold beers to get us safely across the Arabian Sea, but at last we docked in Bombay. The planters wished me good luck, which they obviously thought I needed in such a strange profession, and I went ashore. What a crowded, smelly, jabbering place Bombay was! I was met by Dalton's representative, a shifty little ground type. I should have known better than to trust him to look after my surplus baggage, including the evening tail-coat I had been advised to bring. I never saw it again. I took another boat to Karachi. It was a scruffy coaster, captained by a Greek. Both had seen better days. What a relief it was to see the cheerful face of Ginger Jones amongst the crowd on the dockside at Karachi! He soon had us installed in the local YMCA and introduced me to '*burra-pegs*' – double whisky, usually with soda.

'The beer is bloody awful,' he said. 'Japanese stuff. You'll have to get used to these.'

I didn't see that as being a problem.

The next day he and Andrews took me out to the airport to meet *The Spider*. She was a big single-engined Fokker monoplane, with a roomy cabin that could take twelve passengers in its wicker seats. She was an ideal joy-riding plane, and I liked the look of the large door in the side of the fuselage. It would provide a much more pleasant way for a parachutist to take to the air than clambering out of the cramped cockpit of a tiny biplane.

The Spider had an eventful history. She had belonged to the Duchess of Bedford, and it was in *The Spider*, piloted by Captain Barnard, that 'the Flying Duchess' had made eventful and record-breaking flights to India and Cape Town in 1929 and 1930. She wasn't just a passenger. She had learned to fly in 1926, at the age of sixty. In addition to occasional spells at the controls of *The Spider* during the long flights, the Duchess flew her Gipsy Moth and Puss Moth from her airstrip in the grounds of Woburn Abbey, and in 1933 had won a prize in the Concours d'Elégance at Brooklands. She was a game old bird. Later, in 1937 and at the age of seventy-one, she would climb into her Gipsy Moth Major at Woburn, take off and head north-east, never to be seen again. A few spars from the Moth were washed ashore near Yarmouth. Some would say that she did it deliberately, knowing that her flying licence would not be renewed because of her age ... But in 1934 she was still alive and flying high.

The Duchess had sold *The Spider* to Barnard, and in 1931 he had used it in the first of the large flying circuses to tour Britain, with John Tranum as his wing-walker and parachutist. Now it belonged to Dalton, and we were getting it ready at Karachi for the tour of north-west India.

The airfield at Karachi was one of those plotted by Sir Alan Cobham back in the twenties, when he had been surveying likely routes for Imperial Airways. At that time, it hadn't been decided whether those routes would be flown by airships or aeroplanes. An airship mooring-mast had been built at Karachi to take the R.101, and it was still standing when we were there. Very sad, it looked – as though it was waiting for the big silver ship, wondering where it was. Nobody had told it that the R.101 had blundered into the Beauvais Ridge on its maiden flight to India in 1930, killing all but six of its fifty-four passengers and crew and bringing British airship hopes to a fiery end.

Amongst the RAF types at Karachi, who should I meet but Warrant Officer Kelly, who had been my flight-sergeant on the Comms Flight at Northolt! Hollinghurst had been at Karachi too and had been posted back to Britain only a few days before my arrival. He had read in the newspapers of my involvement in the forthcoming tour and had left regrets at not being there to meet me.

One day, while Andrews and Ginger were working on *The Spider*, and I was painting the wicker seats a bright blue, a sleek, twin-engined job came roaring in from the east and put down on the dusty airfield. It was one of the new De Havilland Comets, built for long-distance air-racing and in this case being flown by Cathcart-Jones and K.H. Waller on the return leg of their thirteen-day record-breaking flight from Britain to Australia and back. They stayed at Karachi just long enough to refuel the plane and grab a few hours rest, then they were roaring into the skies again, racing west. Cathcart-Jones, a former naval pilot, was a regular flier with the air circuses, and later I would get to know him well.

We too were soon off – heading for Lahore in *The Spider*. Later, I would have opportunities to fly the kite myself when Andrews needed a spell, but on this first leg he was at the controls and I was in the right-hand seat, with the map. For some of the flight we could follow the meandering, half-dried watercourses of the Indus, but for much of the time we flew above the parchment-like surface of the Sind desert, with not a recognizable feature in sight. The cockpit was open-sided, without windows, but although there was a fair breeze coming in, it was a hot one. Suddenly, the map was no longer with us. The swirl of warm air had whipped it from my hand and out of the cockpit, and it was now somewhere behind us, fluttering down to the desert. We weren't exactly lost. We just weren't sure where we were. Andrews flew on until we saw a small village off the port wing. He banked *The Spider* towards it and put her down on a boulder-strewn piece of ground. *The Spider* was a robust kite, which was just as well. It was a rough landing.

We were immediately surrounded by villagers, many of whom had never seen an aeroplane before, and certainly not on the ground. They all wanted to touch it, but we managed to keep them from admiring it to pieces. They gave us some idea of the direction and distance of Multan, where we had arranged to take on fuel. When we were reasonably sure that there were no kids hanging on the propeller, we started her up and left the villagers in a cloud of dust, then followed their vague directions.

Multan was an Army base. The great attraction of such places was that only in an Army mess could you get a decent beer – McEwans, shipped out to India as ballast in the troop ships. We were certainly looking forward to being entertained to a cool pint or two. Andrews put the kite down and switched off. We got out and stood in the shade of the wing, waiting for the Army officers to come out and invite us to the mess and the McEwans. Not a soul appeared. Just a bullock cart, ambling out with an uninterested driver and our drum of Burma Shell petrol. The officers were waiting for us to finish the refuelling before taking us for a drink, we decided. So we set to and pumped the petrol up into the tanks – hard work, which made us even thirstier. But nobody came. So we climbed on board, started her up and left Multan and its ghostly garrison and its even more ghostly cold beer and headed north-west for Lahore.

Delayed by the loss of our map and our search for directions and with the land below darkening rapidly, it soon became apparent that we wouldn't reach Lahore before night-fall. No flare-paths in those days. We found what was apparently another Army camp and in rapidly fading light had no alternative but to put down on an adjacent piece of open ground. It turned out to be the polo field, and there was just enough light to show that the tail-skid had torn great lumps out of its carefully prepared surface. This, we thought, would not endear us to the residents. But instead of the indifference of Multan, we were made most welcome by the major in command and by his charming wife and were soon getting outside the cold beer we had been longing for, while servants prepared baths and a meal, and the punkah-wallah punkahed away at a fair old rate. The place, we discovered, was called Sargodha. In the morning a magnificent four-in-hand took us out to *The Spider*. The Army, we decided, weren't such bad types after all.

From Lahore we flew on to Rawalpindi, where we were to start the tour and where we joined up with Captain Dalton and the Tiger Moths that would provide the aerobatics and the stunt flying. The other pilot, Sullivan, hadn't turned up. He never did. We heard the full story later. He had set off from Britain in Dalton's Fox Moth, to fly it to Lahore. His first stop was Paris, where he stayed until he had spent the entire cash-float that Dalton had provided for fuel and emergencies. He wired for some more and blew that lot when he reached Tripoli. Knowing that he wouldn't get any more out of Dalton, he left the Moth there, cadged a lift back to Britain and quietly disappeared for a few months.

We also met Major Dyer, who was acting as Dalton's agent in India. He was a pompous piece of work. As soon as I set eyes on him, I knew that Major Dyer and I were not going to get on very well.

I much preferred 'Mr Smith' who was to be in charge of our local labour force and the servants. 'Mr Smith' was a *'chee-chee'*, as the offspring of white fathers and Indian mothers were called. Most of them had been fathered by the British engineers who had built and run the Indian railways. To me, some of them looked and sounded as British as I did, many of them with fair hair, but the resident whites could tell them a mile off. 'Mr Smith' provided me with my personal bearer, Gulab Khan, and suggested that I pay him 30 rupees a month. That was just over £2, which seemed rather little. The Army officers we met during the tour considered it excessive.

And so, at Rawalpindi, the real business began. Apart from the heat, and the brown earth, and the dark faces, and the fruity smell of India, and the strange language interspersed with English over the public-address system, it was not much different from a British air show. There was the fly-past to start the display; the aerobatics and the stunt flying; the 'bombing' with flour-bags; *The Spider* taking up those who could afford a joy-ride; and the parachute jumps ...

I used the chutes that John Tranum had left in India after the previous tour. They were Irvin-type chutes with standard flat, circular canopies, made of pongee silk, and although they were more porous than normal, there was usually so much heat radiating from the sun-baked ground that the rate of descent of the parachute was comparatively slow. The heat also caused a bit of turbulence, but I could handle that and invariably managed to come in for a stand-up landing. It's always good for the show, that casual arrival on the ground as though you've just stepped from a Rolls Royce instead of fallen from an aeroplane a thousand feet up. In India, however, my stand-up landings were not just in the interests of showmanship. Snakes, I had been told, could be lurking in the most unlikely places, and the Krait – a particularly evil little beggar – was all too common in this part of the country. So I had no intention of rolling about in all that dust and dry grass. I wanted to arrive on my feet, up and ready to run at the first sign of a wriggle.

Those stand-up landings on the hard-baked ground were softened by a pair of boots John Tranum had left with the chutes. Until then I had always jumped in ordinary shoes. These were made for the job, with 'sorbo' inner-soles. Real luxury!

As I had anticipated, jumping from the passenger door of *The Spider* was a treat. There was an unobstructed view of the ground from the high-winged Fokker, so that I could be sure of my dropping-off point. Nice, leaning out of the door into the slipstream, watching the field sliding slowly underneath us, signalling any directions to Andrews as he leaned out of the cockpit looking back at me, then giving him a wave and diving through the wide opening in the fuselage with a wonderful sense of freedom and space. There were usually some paying-passengers in the cabin to watch the foolhardy Englishman hurl himself out of the aircraft, so I tried not to make it look too easy. They were paying to see a dare-devil, not someone who was enjoying himself. The relatively cool rush of air during the few seconds of free fall before I pulled the rip-cord was always welcome.

As soon as I landed, Gulab Khan would come rushing up to gather the chute and carry it off through the crowd, as proud as a father with a babe in his arms. Then he would stand guard and keep the inquisitive away while I repacked it. At many of the places at which we appeared, the natives had never seen an aeroplane, let alone a parachutist, and their curiosity was not easy to control. At Udaipur, for instance, as soon as *The Spider* took off, hordes of locals swarmed onto the field behind it, and it took ages to clear them off so that the kite could land again. Dalton, dashing too and fro on a horse, merely added to the confusion.

Gulab Khan would like to have helped me pack the chutes, but that is something I have never let anybody do. It was my life I was stowing into those packs. What I did let him do was to pick out the camel thorns from the silk. They were vicious things and would have fastened the canopy like safety pins if we hadn't got them out.

Each morning, Gulab Khan would wake me with tea in a porcelain pot, and a dish of fresh papaya. That was nice, but what we really longed for was a glass of decent ale. As Ginger had said, the Japanese chemical stuff was dreadful. *Burra-pegs* were all very well, but oh for a proper beer! In the Chevrolet that Dalton had hired, Ginger and I would sometimes drive miles to the nearest Army unit, there to consume several pints of McEwans.

Although we covered quite a lot of ground during the tour, we didn't move around as frequently as an air circus did in Britain, so there was a bit of time for socializing. However, the social customs and the rigid caste system of India all seemed a bit strange to a Yorkshireman like myself. When we moved on from Rawalpindi to appear at Lahore, we used the Maidan – the central parade ground – as our show field. It was just before Armistice Day, and when I jumped onto the Maidan during the first show, I noticed a right beauty, selling poppies. She was a blonde, beautifully dressed. I made a play for her, and when I was invited to a party at the house of the editor of *The Court and Military Gazette*, I took this girl along with me. I thought the atmosphere was a bit strained but didn't realize why until later in the evening, when the hostess advised me, 'Mr Ward, it isn't done to mix with *chee-chees* ...'

Also at Lahore, at a ball, I bumped into one of the girls I had met on the voyage out. She had been quite free with her favours on board the *Strathaird*, but now she cut me dead. The fact that she was with her husband may have had something to do with it, although I did hear of the lady who froze a former shipboard 'acquaintance' with the words, 'In the circle in which I move, sleeping with a woman does not constitute an introduction.'

Then there were the strange ways in which the Indians treated their own womenfolk. We'd been warned to keep away from the women of the rich nobs for whom we often put on a show. At Kaparthala, I jumped for His Highness the Maharajah Sir Jalbert Singh. An area had been turfed especially for the event, and on a raised and shaded dais His Highness took his place surrounded by a bevy of real beauties, dressed in figure-hugging saris. Most of them, I believe, were French or White Russian. Nobody was allowed near enough to find out. The enclosure was cordoned off with silk ropes and guarded by formidable-looking characters with even more formidable swords. I decided, however, that I would get a closer look at those lovelies. When I jumped, I made sure I left *The Spider* in just the right spot to open my chute a short distance upwind of the enclosure, then I slipped the canopy to land almost at the Maharajah's feet. He was most impressed. So were his ladies. So was I.

I had been so pre-occupied with steering the chute close to the dais that I dropped the rip-cord after I had opened up. Gulab Khan organized a search and offered a one-rupee reward, and it was soon found.

On another occasion, a wealthy landowner asked Dalton if I would jump into the gardens of his country house so that his wives, who were in purdah, could watch. I flew over the place in *The Spider* to look for a suitable landing-spot. The gardens were extensive but complicated by marble pavilions and pathways. There was a lake, with what looked like gray logs lying on the banks. Perhaps I could land in the water? Then I saw one of the logs move. They weren't logs at all: they were crocodiles. Dalton managed to convince the client that parachutists were not easy to replace, and persuaded him to bring his ladies to the airfield very early in the morning and to instal them in a pavilion from which they could see without being seen. Dalton told me that a landing some fifty yards from the pavilion would do very well on this occasion, thank you ...

It was a lot different when I jumped for a party of Parsees, for their women mixed freely and wore elegant dresses and picture hats, like a miniature Ascot. I found all these different customs very confusing.

The pre-occupation with social position wasn't confined to the Indians. At least they based their caste system on religious beliefs, whereas the British had no such excuse. Top of the British pile were the government represen- tatives and the members of the Indian Civil Service. Then came the military, with its own hierarchy, ranging from the Indian cavalry regiments down to the Royal Ordnance Corps and the RAF. Below them were the merchants, themselves subdivided into commerce and trade – the 'box wallahs'. And somewhere below them came Ginger Jones and me, a mere engineer and a crazy parachutist. Every hostess and personal secretary had their own copy of the government-issued 'Warrant of Precedence' which would tell them if a sanitary inspector should be seated higher up the dinner table than an assistant to the district judge. Since the 'Warrant' didn't include professional parachutists, they had no idea where to put me, so I wasn't invited to many dinners.

Dyer certainly saw Ginger and me as a lower order. He treated us like dirt. It came to a head at Kaparthala, where he and Dalton were lodged in splendid comfort in the equivalent of a circuit judge's quarters, at the Maharajah's expense, whilst the rest of us were in the ususal 'dak bungalow' – a government staging-house which offered the bare necessities and where we had to pay for our food. Andrews didn't seem to mind. He was an easy-going type, whereas both Ginger and I were awkward little beggars. We'd had enough. We went to Dyer's accommodation, ordered cigars and a *burra-peg* from his bearer and were settling down to enjoy them when Dyer himself came storming in.

'What do you think you are doing here?' he bellowed in his Indian Army voice.

'We've come to see how the other half live, you fat sod,' said Ginger.

Dyer would have had us flogged if he could.

We got a lot more respect from the natives. At Amritsar, when I was visiting the Golden Temple, I was recognized by a Sikh. He stopped and bowed and said 'You jump from sky with umbrella! You very brave man ... You have heart of tiger.' Dyer, by the way, kept a very low profile while we were at Amritsar. His father had been that General Dyer who during a bit of civil strife in 1919 had given the troops the order to open fire on the civilian crowds in the town's central meeting-place, killing 1,500 men, women and children.

I made several jumps at Amritsar, where we lived in tents outside the town and took excellent meals at the station restaurant. From there we flew to Alwah, across mountainous country that would have offered little opportunity for forced landing had our single engine decided to go on strike. I was thinking that it would have been safer by road until I heard that the coach that had come through the hills with our public-address equipment had been attacked by tribesmen with bows-and-arrows. The driver had some of the arrows to prove it. Alwah was a strange and isolated place, full of peacocks and fakirs. The peacocks were far more attractive than those Hindu holy men and smelled a damn sight sweeter. The local maharajah had recently been deposed for tyrannous behaviour and homosexual excesses, and the place was in the charge of a British Resident. We gave only two shows there, then moved on to Ajmer, where I made three descents onto the polo field of Mayo College, which catered solely for Indian princes.

Udaipur was next. It was a walled city, to which access was made through a single and enormous wooden gate. We were lodged in a hotel outside the walls and were told that if we ventured into the city we were to be sure to be out before sundown, when the gate would be closed and guarded. By the time we had exhausted the delights of the walled city of Udaipur, the sun wasn't just down: it was thinking of coming up again. A certain amount of rupees had to exchange hands before the giant wooden gate swung open to let us out.

I still hadn't encountered any snakes, but there was plenty of alternative livestock about. When Ginger and I went early one morning to check *The Spider* at Udaipur, we noticed what looked like paw-marks in the dust. We mentioned it to Dalton. 'Leopard, I expect. Or panther ...' he said, casually. We thought he was having us on. Then the next day, in the grounds of the maharajah's palace, we saw what looked like a giant rat-trap. Inside was a jet-black panther with the most evil yellow eyes you've ever seen. It almost shook the cage to pieces when it saw us. It had been caught the night before, we were told, and it was undoubtedly the owner of those paw-marks.

When the Maharajah of Udaipur came to the show, he arrived in a magnificent yellow-and-black Rolls Royce with fittings of gold. He may have been rich, but that didn't stop him having a weak bladder: wherever he went, he was followed by the royal commode carried in a black sedan chair.

Then it was Ahmadabad, where we met a bunch of

Lancashire master-weavers who were teaching the trade in the local cotton mills, and with whom we had a *burra-peg* or two in their very pleasant bar. I did four jumps there. One of them was at the local flying club, at night. A local prince owned one of the old-type autogiros with free-rotating vanes, and insisted on showing it off as part of the display. It so delayed my jump that it was dark by the time we were airborne in *The Spider*. Fortunately there was a full moon, so I suppose the spectacle of a white canopy drifting down in the mellow light appeared quite romantic to the lovely Parsee ladies seated on the veranda of the clubhouse. Never mind the romance, I thought – I wasn't being payed to jump at night!

In fact, I wasn't being payed much at all. Just £2 for each jump, and sometimes there was only one of those at each show, for the attendances were poor. At most of the places we visited, the large majority of the locals couldn't afford the 5 annas entry fee, let alone pay for a joy-ride. Oh, the locals would come flocking along when we dropped our publicity leaflets all over the countryside before a show, but they would stop short of the pay-desk. They sat down outside the field and all around it, for there was no screening to obstruct their view. It was poor trade, and the circus was barely covering its expenses. At one show, only one customer turned up for a ride in *The Spider* and was most indignant when Dalton refused to fly him. If any of the maharajahs and princes who attended our shows ever contributed to the gate-money, Ginger and I certainly didn't benefit from it. Nor had all those Indian nobs come forward to pay for a parachute jump under my guidance – just one, at Lahore.

Also, the fun was wearing a bit thin. The mysteries of the Indian caste system and the hypocrisy of the British equivalent were getting on my wick. Although I had little to do with the likes of Dyer, it was still too much, and if I took a shine to a *chee-chee* girl, I didn't want some memsahib telling me it 'wasn't done'. I was fed up with Japanese beer; fed up with *burra-pegs*; fed up with curries; fed up with the heat. I was also beginning to worry that, if I didn't get back to Britain soon, I might miss out on a job with Barker and

King for their British summer tour.

It all blew up at Baroda, where we lived in a hotel with iron bars over the windows to keep the monkeys out. Dalton and the others usually went to the show field before it was necessary for me to appear, and would send one of the Chevrolets back for me. At Baroda, the transport didn't turn up, and I had to hire a *tonga* – one of those little two-wheeled pony-hauled carriages. When I complained to Dalton, he said much too abruptly, 'You could have walked!'

That did it. I quit the India Air Pageant there and then. I always was a bit fiery but probably wouldn't have been so quick off the mark if I hadn't been ready to go in any case.

Dalton was not happy, of course. It was too late for him to get another parachutist, but I don't think that a jumper was making much difference to the number of his paying customers. He gave me a draft for what I was owed and for my passage back to Britain. Baroda was as close as the tour would take us to Bombay, and it was nearly Christmas. If I could get a boat, there would be some fine fun on board over the festive season. A few days later, on 23 December, I was back on board the *Strathaird*.

Sad that it should end like that. It had been fun for a while, and a great experience, and there were no lasting ill-feelings. When I next met Dalton, several years later, he greeted me like a long-lost friend. He told me that, when the tour had ended, he had sold *The Spider* to a wealthy Indian who had allowed it to rot to pieces on a field.

As I had expected, Christmas and New Year on board the *Strathaird* were rolled into one long party. By the time we got to Port Said, I had just about enough cash left to buy a camel-hair overcoat at Simon Artz. It was going to be cold at home.

7

Paying the Price

When I returned – wiser but not much richer – from India, I took up lodgings at the flying-club at Broxbourne. It was inexpensive; good for credit and company; close enough to London's bright lights; and I was on the spot in case any odd jobs came up. They didn't.

Bill Hire was on hand to help pass the time, and we did the town together. He knew his way round the London spots, and only the best was good enough. No more Hammersmith Palais. It was tie-and-tails and into the West End night clubs, where 'bottle parties' were all the rage – and also the latest ruse to circumvent the licensing laws.

Bill was already working on advance publicity for Barker and King. They had ditched the title British Hospitals Air Pageant immediately after the 1934 tour. Too many people were asking just how much of the profit was finding its way into hospitals. 'Jubilee Air Pageant' had a nice patriotic ring to it, and 1935 did just happen to be Jubilee Year. So Jubilee Air Pageant it was to be, under the same management, still with most of the old crew, and still – I was happy to confirm – with Harry Ward as its senior parachutist.

Before the season began, however, I received a nasty shock to the system. I was in the clubhouse at Broxbourne one day when a chap in a bowler hat came in, asking for Mr Ward.

'That's me,' I said, 'Harry Ward.' I thought he had brought me something. A legacy, perhaps? Or the offer of a job? It was neither of those. It was an income tax demand. The miserable types had caught up with me at last.

Sadly, there were even greater hazards in aviation at

that time than tax inspectors. The 1935 season was to take a heavy toll of circus jumpers and fliers. First to go was my friendly rival, John Tranum.

I had come to know John a little better since our first meeting at the Russell factory. Our paths had crossed at several air shows, first of all during the 1933 season when I noticed that he was wearing suede shoes and no socks. It wasn't long before Harry Ward was walking out in suede shoes and no socks. As I had begun to make my own name as a parachutist, I no longer needed to copy John Tranum, and our respect had become mutual. Although there was intense rivalry amongst professional jumpers for whatever jobs and rewards were going, there was also a great bond of companionship. We shared the same unique sensations and the same risks. John Tranum and I had even shared the same boots. We didn't have to be close friends to know each other well.

Tranum had given up jumping for the Russell Company and, in addition to his exhibition work, had taken a job as demonstration jumper for Leslie Irvin. It was Irvin who persuaded him to try for a new free-fall record. The longest recorded drop had lasted seventy-five seconds, made in 1931 by the American 'Spud' Manning, over Los Angeles. By that time, of course, the old myth that free fall would kill had been well and truly buried, but very little was known about *how* to fall free. Arthur East had been well on the way to mastering body flight when he was killed, and 'Spud' Manning was another of the very few who by trial and error had learned how to stabilize the falling body and to use the limbs as control surfaces. Most jumpers who went for the high ones didn't even try. The trouble with spreading your arms and legs out in free fall is that, if you don't get it right – which means symmetrical – you turn yourself into a fair resemblance of a four-bladed propeller and can be sent flailing round in a flat spin that is certainly unpleasant and potentially lethal. Better, thought most jumpers, to keep the legs together and the arms across the chest, and to accept the gentle somersaults and head-down rotations that usually occurred as the body accelerated in this attitude to 120 mph. That was how John

Tranum fell for more than eighty seconds when he jumped from a Hawker Hart at 21,000 feet over Netheravon in May 1933, with a stopwatch held in the palm of his hand, in front of his face. He never attempted to stabilize his fall.

A few months later, the Russian parachutist Ievdokimov beat the Tranum jump with a free fall from 26,000 feet. The pressure was on John to regain the world record. Arrangements were made for him to leap from 30,000 feet at Copenhagen in early March 1935.

I don't think that John Tranum ever wanted to do that second high one. He never enjoyed those long drops. He made no secret of that. He was a man who liked to be in control of what he was doing in the air, and he usually was, which is why he had survived so many crazy stunts. But he wasn't in control of free fall, and those long, helpless tumbles from high altitude must have worried him. Had he discovered free-fall stability, it would have been different, but he was never to experience the supreme elation of a controlled drop. By 1935 he was a frightened jumper. That is the time to quit. He didn't.

On 7 March, at Kastrup, he climbed into a cockpit for the last time. The Danish military plane climbed slowly over Copenhagen towards 30,000 feet and that world record. At 27,000 feet, John Tranum made frantic signs to the pilot, Captain Laerum, who realized that something was desperately wrong and put the kite into a steep dive towards Kastrup. When they lifted John Tranum from the plane, he was dead. From a heart attack. From fear.

The death of Ivor Price was more spectacular. He was once again Cobham's senior parachutist for the National Aviation Day tour. Like me, he had a second jumper now – Naomi Heron-Maxwell, one of the threadbare gentry and quite a girl, who would survive her parachuting career to become an outstanding glider pilot. Ivor was a popular and pleasant chap. I believe he intended to retire from the jumping game before long, for he had told me when I first met him in 1933 that he was saving up to buy a riding-stable. He had also married, two weeks before he died.

Ivor was a very tidy man, and it was being tidy that killed him. Whenever he was packing his chute and had reached the stage of straightening the lines, he used to tie a handkerchief round the bunched cords just below the periphery, to keep them neatly in place while he pleated the canopy. It made a very smart job of it. But at Woodford, on 30 May, he forgot to untie the handkerchief.

He and Naomi were doing a double jump from a pair of Avro Cadets. They went out at 2,000 feet. Naomi's chute streamed and opened; Ivor's just streamed. The mouth of the canopy was locked tight by that forgotten handkerchief, and he whistled straight in, right in front of the crowd. The announcer, for once, was lost for words, so he played the National Anthem over the loudspeakers. Poor Ivor! He would have had a few seconds to think about it, and I have often wondered if he realized what he had done.

Naomi Heron-Maxwell stayed on the tour, and Ivor's place was taken by Marsland – who had also replaced me after my injury on the 1933 tour with Cobham. He was never a regular jumper but something of an odd-job man around the flying circuses, ready to have a go at anything. When he took Ivor's place, he didn't last very long. Cobham had always thought that lift-off jumps were more spectacular than short free drops, and often had his jumpers pull off from the wing of the Clive. For once I disagreed with Sir Alan. It was that brief sight of a body falling free, and that moment of wondering if the chute would ever open, that thrilled the crowds. But mostly I disagreed because a lift-off with the Lobe was a recipe for disaster. The Irvin, with its pilot-chute, was ideal for the job, but when the Lobe came out of its pack, it didn't have a sky-hook like that to drag it clear and straighten it out. There was a great risk, I believed, of the canopy's becoming entangled with the lines, or of the body's rolling into it. That's what happened to Marsden. He hurtled down from a thousand feet with the Lobe wrapped round him like a silken shroud.

In case anyone should think that jumping out of

aeroplanes was any more dangerous than flying them, the circuses were also struck by several fatal aircraft crashes during the '35 season. At Bodmin, our 'Andy' Anderson – for reasons we shall never know – spun into the ground. With him died his mechanic and the son of the Mayor of Bodmin Town, who was up for his first and last flip. Cobham lost an ace glider pilot, Collins, when his machine shed a wing during an inverted loop. At Blackpool, towards the end of his tour, tragedy really hit the Cobham circus when pilots Stewart and Carruthers collided in mid-air. Carruthers managed to land his kite, but Stewart was killed with his two girl passengers, and a blind man who was in the house onto which the plane crashed.

We mourned briefly the loss of good friends, learned what we could from their mistakes, were perhaps a little more cautious for a few days (the way you are when you drive past someone else's car crash on the road), then carried on as normal. Risk was our business. It was what we sold to the public. They didn't come along to see how *safe* it all was. We did what we could to reduce the hazards without its being too obvious, but we had to retain the image and some of the reality of danger. And what is life without a bit of risk, anyway? Beer would never have tasted so good; pound notes would never have felt so crisp; and girls would never have looked so pretty, were it not for the risks we daily ran.

A reserve parachute might have saved Ivor Price, if he could have flown it without its becoming tangled with his streamer to create what was known in the trade as a 'Roman candle'. Yet none of us ever seriously considered carrying a second chute. That was not because we were imprudent. It was because we had confidence in ourselves and our kit. If we had taken to wearing a reserve, it would have been because we were frightened, and if you become frightened in the jumping game, you don't just buckle on a chest-type insurance policy: you get out. That is what John Tranum should have done. As for poor Ivor, I would never find myself in his situation because I didn't do daft things like tie a handkerchief round my rigging-lines. Arthur East had taught me well. Also, I had spent several years packing for other people, and that makes you even more careful than when you are packing for yourself. The RAF had instilled in me a sense of self-discipline and orderly thinking that was probably the reason for my survival as a professional jumper at a time when so many of my contemporaries were quite literally biting the dust. All that square-bashing, all the 'bull', all those hours of tedious but meticulous instruction in the trade training school at Manston – that hadn't been wasted time. It had provided me with a mental survival kit.

The 1935 season wasn't all doom and gloom. Far from it! Despite the occasional tragedies, we remained a jovial crew as we flew and jumped our way once more round the British Isles. A welcome and lively addition to the team was former Navy pilot Owen Cathcart-Jones. He and A.K. Waller had flown one of the De Havilland Comets in the celebrated MacRobertson Race from Britain to Melbourne in 1934. Although they hadn't won the race, they had established a record for the round trip to Australia and back, and I had first met 'C.J.' during his brief stop at Karachi on the return flight. He mostly flew the Short Scion for us, and a constant companion for a while was a glamorous blonde, Miss Niesen, who was a KLM pilot. C.J. was a dapper little man, and wherever he was, there was a good-looking woman not far away. When we were rained off at Chester, I recall that we booked the front row of the local theatre for the evening. C.J. took a shine to one of the chorus-girls and in the middle of the show sent her a note via the drummer, with a fiver to help it on its way. That was C.J. – known as 'The Deb's Delight'.

Then there was Richmond Fotheringay Robinson, another of our pilots, 'Robbie' for short. I went into a gents' outfitters with him when he was looking for a new pair of flannels. When a female assistant brought a pair, he stripped off the ones he was wearing there and then. The assistant nearly died of fright. He had forgotten to put any underpants on that morning, and his shirt was very short. He didn't bat an eyelid. With a name like Richmond Fotheringay Robinson, you can get away with anything.

Poker took up a lot of our spare time. Too much of it, on occasion. I remember playing until dawn in the Atlantic Hotel in County Cork. The proprietor had joined us, and by the time the sun came up we had won the contents of his tills and had used some of it to cash cheques for him.

During that tour of Ireland I flew with Joe King across the beauty of Galway Bay to take copies of *The Irish Press* to the Aran Isles. Joe tried to put the plane down on the beach, but the sand was too soft, and we landed instead on rough pasture at Inishmore. We were a novelty. Few on the island had ever seen an aircraft that close, and we attracted a number of the natives. I tried to take a photograph of the girls in their traditional shawls, but they turned their backs. Perhaps it was because the priest was there. He offered us a drink of the local 'poteen' but, knowing its reputation and with forty miles of open sea between us and Galway, we declined. He blessed us, and the Avro, none the less.

On that same tour, Jock Bonar and I paid a visit to the Earl of Bandon, who was a squadron-leader currently on leave from the RAF. He had been taught to fly by Jock, who had been a sergeant pilot in the RAF during the 1920s. Jim Mollinson had been another of Jock's pupils. The Bandons' mansion had been burned down during 'The Troubles', and he and his lady were living in their agent's house, where they made us most welcome. In the morning his gamekeeper took me to a river that was stuffed with fish. I didn't catch one. He showed me how to cast, but I kept hooking trees instead of fish.

I never was any good at those 'county' sports. Jimmy King took me riding once. We were at Hertfordingbury and went early in the morning to nearby stables. Jimmy, who was an ex-cavalryman, had riding-breeches and all the gear. I wore flannels and shirt. My horse was a big black brute – so big that Jimmy had to lever me onto it. The stable boss led us down a lane, where my suggestion that he should fit his horses with mudguards didn't strike him as being at all funny. When we came through a gate into an open field, the other two went away at a gallop, and my mount, despite all my efforts to hold him, took off after them. There I was, lying full length along its back, feet out of the stirrups, flannels up round my knees, thumbs hooked into the rings of its bit. 'Do you always ride like that?' Jimmy King asked. I walked like the Hunchback of Notre Dame for days after that ride. And they say parachuting is dangerous!

Bill Hire was turning out to be a good jumper, and during the season I undertook the training of another young volunteer. When we were appearing at Wallingford, Jimmy agreed to take on – as a general helper – a young fellow from a local 'Home of Correction for Young Gentlemen'. Waugh was his name. We thought that a few parachute jumps might be good for his soul. He showed all the healthy fear of it but came through his first few jumps all right and might have become quite a good parachutist if he hadn't run into a bit of bad luck at a time when such things can put you off for life. His first piece of bad luck was in the shape of a tall tree at Pitlochry. He took a bad knock and was unconscious when we got him down from the branches. A few days later, at Peebles, he landed in the River Tweed and came close to drowning. We agreed that he seemed to have an uncertain future in the parachuting trade, so he made no more jumps. But he was a nice lad, and I think he benefited from his season with the circus. His parents certainly thought so and were most grateful to us. He 'went straight' after he left us, stayed in the aviation world and eventually became a good pilot.

Those Scottish fields, I suppose, were not the best training-grounds for novice jumpers. Even I found some of them a bit tight. For the two jumps that I made at Renfrew, in order to land in front of the public enclosure I had to drift right in over the cemetery. I was mindful of the great American wing-walker and jumper Wesley May, who, when jumping for Gates' Flying Circus, had landed in a cemetery. Actually he landed in a tree, but then fell out of it, broke his back on a tombstone and died in hospital. So I made sure that I cleared that graveyard in Renfrew.

Even so, I didn't get through the Jubilee Air Pageant tour without a few bumps and bruises of my own, and the odd scare or two. On Bodmin on the same day that 'Andy' Anderson died, I almost bought it myself. My Lobe had one of those sticky openings – so sticky that I thought it wasn't going to open at all, but it eventually inflated with a most welcome bang when I was about a hundred feet from the deck.

I had another bad one at Castle Douglas. As I ripped at 700 feet, I knew as soon as I felt the chute deploying and dragging at my shoulders that something was going wrong up there. Sure enough, when I got my head back and looked up, instead of that lovely round umbrella, flying above me was what looked like a giant brassière. The canopy had turned inside out and was divided into two separate lobes by the four centre lines passing over it. I wasn't able to shift them and came spiralling down at a rate of knots. I knew that my legs would be stoved in if I landed feet-first at that speed. I watched the ground come rushing and revolving upwards, and just before it hit me I pulled hard on the liftwebs to swing my legs sideways and take the impact on my backside and shoulders. I was badly bruised, but nothing was broken. The crowd loved it.

At Harrow I broke a couple of ribs and jumped for a while with them heavily taped. At Guildford I crunched in rather hard and fractured a bone in my foot. I needed a plaster cast for that one, and jumped with it for several weeks, landing on the good foot. 'Ladies and gentlemen!' bellowed our announcer. 'Harry Ward – the only one-legged parachutist in the world ...' I think Jimmy King was quite sorry when the plaster cast came off and he only had a normal jumper on the programme.

One of the greatest tragedies to befall me during the '35 tour happened at Lincoln. I lost one of John Tranum's boots. I had brought them back from India with me and had grown very accustomed to them. I could have had another pair made, I suppose, but it wouldn't have been the same, so it was back to the shoes.

Towards the end of any tour, tiredness and over-familiarity began to have their effect. I never neglected the essentials. My packing was always meticulous, and I always made sure that I was in a good body position before I pulled that rip-cord. Look after the chute and give it a good chance to go about its business without any interference, and not much can go wrong. In less important matters, however, I suppose I became rather blasé – like dropping off in not quite the right place. If the surrounds of the field were potentially lethal, I certainly made no mistake, but in more open countryside I was sometimes a bit lazy. At Dartford I landed in the grounds of a lunatic asylum. The attendants thought I should stay there. Somewhere else in the south-east I landed to polite applause in the middle of a cricket match.

The most serious damage that I suffered during the 1935 season, however, was not to my person but to my pocket. We were at Newmarket. Naturally enough, we fell in with a bunch of jockeys, including the great Harry Wragg. In the strictest confidence, he gave us a red-hot tip for the next day's racing. We put our shirts on it. It was beaten out of sight. Now that *was* a tragedy ...

8

Tom Campbell-Black's Air Display

The 'big names' in aviation during the 1930s were not always the best fliers. Fame as a pilot was a product of sponsorship and publicity, as much as of flying skill. To become known outside the aviation circle, you had to win one of the major races, or break an existing record, or create a new 'first flight' to some increasingly distant part of the globe. Flying a couple of thousand passengers out of tiny fields and doing a spot of crazy flying to keep the customers happy didn't hit the headlines. If you killed yourself, of course, you might get a mention in the local press. The long-distance merchants were undoubtedly brave and competent fliers, but not all deserved the extravagant applause heaped on them by press and public. In terms of actually handling an aeroplane, for example, Amy Johnson and Amelia Earhart – the most famous names in women's aviation – couldn't hold a candle to the likes of Winifred Spooner and Pauline Gower, who had both learned their trade in the circus game. Jim Mollinson was another who made some great flights but whose success was built largely on luck, whiskys and a short-lived marriage to Amy Johnson.

One of the fliers whose reputation needed no inflation was Tom Campbell-Black. He had been one of the earliest and most able of the East African bush-pilots, flying uncharted country where mechanical failure, poor piloting or navigational error could spell disaster. He was an outstanding flying instructor: Beryl Markham, first woman to fly the Atlantic solo from east to west, had been one of his pupils. When he came to Britain, he did some circus work and other commercial flying and in 1934 teamed up with C.W.A. Scott for the MacRobertson Air Race. What an event that was! Not only was it the greatest air race ever staged but it marked a major turning-point in aviation by confirming the superiority of the monoplane over the biplane. Amongst the twenty machines that took off from Mildenhall for the race to Melbourne were three of the sleek De Havilland Comets, the forerunner of the Mosquito of World War II. Perhaps even more significant was the appearance of the new breed of American airliner, the Douglas DC-2, from which the military Dakota would spring, and the Boeing 247-D which was piloted to Australia by the great American speed and circus fliers Roscoe Turner and Clyde 'Upside-Down' Pangbourne. The race was won by the Comet *Grosvenor House* in just under twenty-one hours – flown by C.W.A. Scott and Tom Campbell-Black. It was front-page stuff.

In 1935 Campbell-Black hit the headlines again, rather painfully this time. Flying another Comet – called *Boomerang* in the hope that it would always come back – he and co-pilot J.G. MacArthur set out to crack the Cape Town record. They took off from Hatfield and, because there was so little space in the tiny racing plane, they decided to fly without parachutes. Who needed parachutes? The space could be better used for stowing a couple of warm overcoats. At the last moment, Campbell-Black's wife, the actress Florence Desmond, persuaded him to change his mind. Out came the overcoats, in went two Irvin seat-packs. Just as well. After a record flight to Cairo of eleven hours ten minutes, the Comet's engines packed in while they were flying over thick bush country in the Sudan. There was nowhere to put the plane down. They had to jump for their lives. They only just made it. When they jettisoned the cockpit cover, the inrush of air pinned them to their seats, and the aircraft went into a nose-down spin. MacArthur was eventually flung out with height to spare, but when Tom Campbell-Black managed to force himself out of the whirling cockpit, he was only a few hundred feet from the ground. He yanked the rip-cord, and the Irvin did its stuff, opening up and putting him down unhurt almost in the same breath, just yards away from the hole in the ground that held the wreckage of *Boomerang*. They arrived at Atbara several days later, by camel, and most grateful to Leslie Irvin and Florence Desmond.

The 'big names' were obvious attractions at air shows, and during 1935 Campbell-Black and Scott had made guest appearances at the circuses. In 1936 they became figureheads of rival tours.

Sir Alan Cobham had decided to leave the circus game at the end of his 1935 season. He wanted to concentrate on his new venture of air-to-air refuelling, and it is also likely that he had the foresight to realize ahead of most of us that the days of the commercial air display were numbered. He sold his flying circus to C.W.A. Scott. When Barker and Jimmy King heard of this, they countered by inviting Tom Campbell-Black to give his name to their own outfit. It needed a new title in any case, for 'Jubilee Air Pageant' was now old hat. So for 1936 we became Tom Campbell-Black's Air Display. 'T.C.B.' himself would put in an appearance whenever he could, but it was the name that was important.

Jimmy King brought together much the same crew as in previous years, except that we had a new senior pilot and a new senior engineer. Very attractive they were, too – Pauline Gower and Dorothy Spicer, a couple of stunning blondes. Nobody had any qualms about working with this particular pair of women, for they had been in circus flying longer than most of us. Both were qualified pilots from the Stag Lane 'stable' and in 1931 were already selling joy-rides from a field near Wallingford. In 1932 they had flown for the Crimson Fleet circus, and in 1933 for British Hospitals Air Pageant, so they were well known to many of the present crew. During the summers of 1934 and '35 they had operated from a fixed base at Hunstanton, putting on shows and selling joy-rides to holiday-makers, and during the actual Jubilee weekend in 1935 they had joined us for a few days in the Midlands, where I had first met them.

Although they had both begun as pilots, early in their

partnership Dorothy Spicer had decided to concentrate on engineering, Pauline on the flying. By 1936, Dorothy Spicer was the only woman to hold the Air Ministry A, B, C and D licences for aircraft engineering, while Pauline Gower, in addition to her pilot's B licence, held the certificate for navigation and a wireless-operator's licence. Recognition of her standing as an aviator would come in 1940, when she was chosen to command the Women's Section of the Air Transport Auxiliary, the famous 'ferry pilots' of the Second World War.

No, we had no doubts about Dorothy Spicer and Pauline Gower: they were a grand pair. They also brought with them their own parachutist, Bruce Williams. Bruce was an actor by profession. He specialized in pantomime, in which he usually played the Demon King, a part which required him to be launched up through a trap-door in the stage floor by what was known as a 'star trap'. Apparently it needed some agility and split-second timing if the performer was to avoid a cracked skull. He had also done some stunt work for the film industry.

Bruce had introduced himself to Pauline Gower and Dorothy Spicer at their Hunstanton base in 1934. 'What you need,' he had said, 'is a parachutist. And I am he.' They hadn't argued, and he had jumped for them at weekends and on holidays throughout their 1934 and '35 seasons. Jumping that regularly into a field only 200 by 300 yards in size, bordered on one side by the main railway line between Hunstanton and King's Lynn, had made a good parachutist of him. He made a welcome addition to our little team of jumpers.

Bruce used one of the relatively new 'GQ' chutes. There weren't many of them around. Like the Russell Company, Gregory & Quilter – despite a great deal of lobbying and publicity – had been unable to break the Irvin monopoly. It would need the immense demand for chutes created by World War II to do that. The GQ was, in fact, as similar to the Irvin as it could be without infringing patent rights. It incorporated the comfort of a pilot-chute, so noticeably lacking in the Lobe. On the other hand, it shared the tendency of the Irvin to oscillate in flight. For the time being, I stayed with the Russell chute. The two made a nice contrast whenever Bruce and I put on a double jump for the 'race to the ground'.

Both Bruce Williams and Bill Hire operated on the understanding that I was the chief parachutist and would still get my retainer and my two jumps a day. They would get anything else that was going, including the double jumps, and would also stand in for me if I happened to be away. They picked up enough to keep them happy, and I was pleased to have the back-up.

The fact that the circus could sustain three parachutists was an indication of the changing attitude towards flying. Increasingly, the circuses were relying on thrills and dare-devilry to pull the crowds. Joy-riding was no longer the novelty it had once been. Whereas the flying display had originally served to attract customers into the passenger queues, it was now becoming more of an end in itself, and parachuting in particular could still pull them in. People would still flock to watch some crazy bloke risk his life. And if instead of a crazy bloke there was a crazy *girl*, they would come in even greater numbers. The history of show-jumping since the early ballooning days is full of pretty girls whose husbands or fathers have put them on the aerial stage while they have stood on the ground collecting the money. On this basis, before the 1936 season began, I had sought to add a touch of feminine charm to our parachute team. I had failed ...

Perhaps I should have paid more attention to John Tranum's experience of teaching the fair sex to parachute. In California, during the twenties, he had taken a girl up for a jump from a thousand feet, using a static-line-operated chute. She was chirpy enough on the ground but at drop height was looking decidedly ill. 'About the colour of the underside of a shark,' John said. She managed to climb onto the wing, but when he yelled at her to jump, she let go of the strut only to grab the static line and slither down it until she was clinging partly to the line and partly to the wing. There she hung, ignoring his curses and his yells to let go. She hadn't the strength to haul herself back onto the wing, and Tranum couldn't leave the controls to help her. He was having trouble enough already, trying to hold the kite while she was flailing around outside. So he took off his safety belt, took careful aim and swiped her across the knuckles with the buckle. She disappeared with a yell. The static line did its work, the girl landed safely and John Tranum never attempted to train another female jumper.

As I said, I didn't have quite the same problem. The first girl I trained was a 21-year-old from Derby, Josephine-Anne Stainton-Nadin. Her father had approached Jimmy King to see what the chances were of making a circus jumper of his daughter, and Jimmy had referred him to me. I agreed to train her for £10 a jump. During the winter of 1935-6, I had taken a temporary job maintaining parachutes for the Royal Air Force Volunteer Reserve at the Blackburn Company's airfield at Brough, near Hull. From there, I borrowed an Irvin seat-pack and arranged with the Doncaster Flying Club to use their airfield and to drop the girl from one of their planes in early March.

Josephine-Anne was a right pet, and her father was a very sensible man to keep such a close eye on her all the time I was teaching her to be a parachutist. She certainly looked the part when I had her all kitted up in white overalls and a leather flying-helmet, and she smiled very prettily at the press photographers I had invited along. She wasn't smiling at 2,000 feet though. But she was a game lass: she gave it a go and came down safely enough. It was a Saturday, and the field was right alongside Doncaster Rovers' football ground, where 14,000 fans had a free parachute show. Josephine-Anne made three jumps but enjoyed none of them and decided that the life of a circus jumper was, after all, not for her.

That trip to Doncaster brought my job at Brough to a premature end. The day off and the loan of the seat-pack had been entirely unofficial, and I got the tip-off that the boss was highly displeased. I've never fancied being given the sack, so I went to see him before I was sent for.

'I'm packing this job in,' I told him.

'You've just beaten me to it,' he said.

I selected my next pupil with more care. I wanted

someone whose nerve had already been tested and proven. Who better than 'Speedy' Pepper? 'Speedy' was already an established circus artiste of the ground-borne variety – a well-known trick-motorcyclist, in fact. Not only did she ride a motorbike round the 'Wall of Death', she did it with a lion sitting in the side-car. Surely I had found the perfect lady parachutist? 'Speedy' did just one jump.

'You're not getting me up there again!' she said afterwards. 'That's bloody dangerous!' And back she went to the safety of 'the Wall of Death' and the lion in the side-car.

Like John Tranum, I didn't train any more girls. A novelty that I introduced with more success in 1936 was to jump with wings, but that is a separate story ...

I almost came a cropper before the 1936 season had even begun. We were always on the look-out for new kites to put into the show – the stranger the better, and they didn't come much stranger than the 'Flying Drone'. It was one of a breed of miniature aeroplanes that it was thought might popularize flying, as the Morris-8 was expected to popularize motoring. Mignet's 'Flying Flea' was perhaps the best known, and 'Dotty' Doig flew one of them for us for a while. The Drone was a single-seater, powered by a Douglas motorcycle engine. It was more like a motorized glider than a conventional aeroplane and was easy to fly. I had kept my pilot's licence current by flying each winter at Broxbourne, and Jimmy King now asked me if I would pick up a Drone from Hanworth and fly it to Broxbourne, where we were to have a couple of days for rehearsal before opening the tour at Luton.

'You'll need a map,' he said.

'No, I won't,' I told him. I'd covered North London in the air and on the ground until I knew it like the back of my hand.

So off I went to Hanworth, where the Austrian gliding ace Kronfeld was manufacturing the Drone, and flew this funny little kite to Broxbourne, where Jock Bonar and several of the others tried it out. They didn't think much of it. OK for parachuting types to stooge around in, they decided, but it wasn't for *real* pilots ... So it was left for me to fly it over to Luton for the first show. When I checked it out, however, I found that there was a slight leak in the petrol tank. It would have to go back for repairs, so I set off for Hanworth instead. It was only a short hop. I thought there would be enough fuel to feed both the engine and the leak, but just north of Enfield the motor died. I was at 1,500 feet. I was aware that the Drone had a fairly flat glide and decided to make for a golf course I could see in the distance. As I passed over a village, I was rather surprised to find myself on a level with the church steeple – whose weather-cock, I noticed, badly needed re-gilding. I wasn't going to make that golf course after all. I gave the kite hard right rudder and opposite aileron to bring it round in a flat turn towards the local allotments, and plonked it down in a potato patch. One wheel was ripped off and a hole was torn in the wing, but the potatoes and I were OK.

We didn't, after all, take the Drone on tour, but when we were appearing at Hereford in early May, a visiting pilot brought his own Drone in and let me have a flip in it. I had been up for about five minutes when I put it into a tight turn and suddenly felt the rudder bar disappear from beneath my feet. The seat had slipped back. It was jammed, and I couldn't bring it forward again. Unable to reach the rudder bar, I managed to get the thing down by using the stick. I told the owner about the seat, and he said he would fix it right away. I don't think he did. Or if he tried, he didn't fix it very well. Later that afternoon, young Cadic, who flew passengers for us in T.C.B.'s own Short Scion five-seater, also took the Drone up. As he took off, he waved to Pauline Gower and Dorothy Spicer, who were sitting on the grass by their Spartan. A few seconds later, at some 400 feet, the Drone flipped into a spin and whistled straight in. They lifted poor Cadic out of the wreckage, and he was rushed off in the ambulance but died in hospital shortly afterwards. I reckon that seat killed him.

We had even more troubles just over a week later, at Coventry. My word, the crowd got their thrills and spills that day! A huge storm cloud built and lingered in the area all afternoon. Although it never came to sit directly over us, it was close enough to play absolute havoc with the winds. You never knew from which direction and at what strength they would be coming, from one minute to the next. The Short Scion was the first victim. Michelmore was flying it. He started his take-off run into a headwind that suddenly became a tailwind. He was heading straight for the hedge. He just managed to lift the plane over it but clipped a wheel, which went spinning off into the next field. We all gathered to watch him fly a couple of circuits, knowing that he was going to have to put it down on one wheel, with a full load of passengers. We probably felt a lot worse about it than he did as we watched him come gliding in for the landing. One slight misjudgement would send the Scion cartwheeling to destruction, but circus pilots in that sort of situation didn't make 'slight misjudgements', and he held it on one wheel until the speed and the wing finally dropped. With a rather unpleasant grinding sound, the plane tilted and slewed and came to a halt right in front of the enclosure, just as though it was all part of the show. The undercarriage and the bottom of the fuselage were wrecked, but pilot and passengers walked away unhurt. Later the insurance company presented Michelmore with a silver cigarette-case for having saved them a tidy sum.

Accident number two of that afternoon happened a few minutes later. Young Dean, one of our mechanics, became a little careless when swinging a prop. It hit his arm and broke it.

Accident number three came within the hour, when the winds played another cruel trick. Pauline Gower thought that she was taking off into wind. So did another pilot, from a completely different direction. They met in the middle of the field. Again, nobody was killed, but the Spartan was wrecked, and Pauline was hit on the head by the wheel of the other plane. It put her into hospital for a month, but it took that wheel right off the axle. A hard-headed girl, our Pauline.

I don't mind admitting that when Bruce Williams and I went up to finish that particular show with our double drop and a 'race to the ground', we didn't race too hard. We didn't want to join the list of that day's casualties, so just made sure that we watched those dodgy winds and got ourselves down safely. Not a good day, at Coventry – except for the spectators, of course. They loved it.

Accidents, however, were not our main problem during the 1936 tour. It was the weather that caused most of our grief. That storm at Coventry was just one of many occasions when it turned against us. The season had begun in April with strong winds from the north-east, sweeping snow and sleet across the country and completely wiping out some of our early shows. The bad weather continued into a dreadful summer. It not only kept the customers away and restricted our flying shows but played havoc with our movement about the country, both by road and by air. Some of those flights from one show to the next, in low cloud and poor visibilty, often across 'Gremlin Country' like the Pennines or the Scottish hills, and with a tiny, fog-shrouded field at the end of it, were hairy. Some of the best flying in the air-circus business went quite unseen by the public.

Tom Campbell-Black flew with us whenever he could, and joined us for most weekends. Sometimes he brought his wife, Florence Desmond, and another actress called Greta Gynnt, and they brightened the place up no end. Nobody could handle a Puss Moth like T.C.B., yet he was the most unassuming of the many great fliers I have met.

But business was not good for Tom Campbell-Black's Air Display. It wasn't just the awful weather. Even on fine days, the crowds were not there as they had been in previous years. At the time, we didn't fully understand why. Because we were still so involved in the excitement and risk of flying, and because for us little had changed, perhaps we were slow to realize that, for the public, some of the adventure and much of the novelty were going out of flying. It was becoming rather more serious. Although nobody really believed that there would be a war, the RAF was at last being expanded: just in case. Also, in 1935, householders had received through their letter-boxes a leaflet telling them what to do in the case of air raids. Air raids? Flying was supposed to be fun, wasn't it?

Another sign of the times had been De Havilland's announcement in 1935 that they were ceasing production of open-cockpit Moths. Cockpits were closing in on us. The romantic image of the goggled flier with his scarf streaming in the prop-wash would soon be a thing of the past! Yes, the fun was fading, and so were the crowds.

Although few people in Britain paid much attention to what was happening in Spain during the summer of 1936, there were reports that the aeroplane was already going to war again. German and Italian aircraft had transported Franco's rebel army from Morocco at the start of the Civil War, and bombers and fighters would surely be used. It was not long before Tom Campbell-Black became involved on the fringes of that conflict.

He had accepted a particularly handsome charter fee to deliver an aeroplane to the rebel forces in Spain, in secret. Oh yes, he was told, there would be a passenger. The passenger turned out to be the rebel leader Marques Rivas de Linares, and T.C.B. duly delivered him to Franco's headquarters at Burgos. Unfortunately, passenger and pilot had been recognized during a refuelling stop while flying down through France, and T.C.B. became a wanted man in Republican Spain. He managed to flee the country by car after anxious moments at numerous road-blocks. It made a good story for the *News of the World*, and the publicity did Tom Campbell-Black's Air Display no harm at all.

In a more indirect way, the Spanish Civil War almost killed Pauline Gower. She was back with us, flying a new Spartan which was piloted from the front cockpit instead of the rear, which meant that she couldn't see any mischief the passengers might get up to. We were at Kirkcaldy, and she was flying over the town with a couple of joy-riders when, without warning, the elevators jammed. She couldn't haul back on the stick at all. She screwed her neck round to look at the tail assembly. The elevator controls seemed to be stuffed with paper. She needed all her skill to put the Spartan down in one piece, and when she had landed, she taxied right up to some of our crew and yelled at them to grab her 'passengers'. It turned out that one of them was a Communist, who had chosen Pauline's aircraft to bombard Kirkcaldy with more than a thousand leaflets depicting 'Fascist Murder of the Spanish Proletariat'. He was subsequently fined £3 for imperilling the safety of an aeroplane.

As we came towards the final weeks of the tour, we saw less of T.C.B. After his Spanish adventure, he became busy with preparations for another air race which it was hoped would create as much interest as the MacRobertson event. It was the Johannesburg Race, inaugurated by T.W. Schlessinger, to start from Portsmouth on 29 September. T.C.B. was planning a solo attempt, flying a Percival Mew Gull, a sleek, single-engined monoplane, and one of the fastest things in the air. Sadly, he didn't live to fly that race, nor to see the end of the circus tour that had carried his name round Britain ...

On 18 September he flew to Speke airport for the Gull to be officially named *Miss Liverpool*. After the well-publicized ceremony, he waved to the crowd and taxied out for take-off. He probably never saw the aircraft that killed him. It was a Hawker Hart of the RAF. Landing into the sun and with limited downward vision, its pilot didn't see the Gull, either. The Hart came down on top of the small monoplane, and its propeller sliced through the canopy and through Tom Campbell-Black.

He was one of the greatest fliers and one of the nicest men I ever knew.

9

Not Exactly a Film Star

All of us were ready for a holiday after that 1936 season. I put away my wings (more about them later) until the next year's tour, and took off for Scotland with Jock Bonar and his wife. Air-show crowds can pall after a while, and we thought there wouldn't be too many of them on the Isle of Arran. We drove north, taking our time, and crossed to the island by ferry. I was just getting used to doing not very much at all when Cathcart-Jones rang. Would I return to London immediately, to discuss some business with him?

No professional jumper could afford to turn his nose up at even the slightest whiff of a job. This was particularly the case at the end of the 1936 season, for financially it had not been a good one. Even in the good times, we air-circus types had our fun and worked hard for one half of the year, and spent the other half wondering if our cash would last us until we went on the road again. It was a bit like hibernating: living off our fat during the winter, and sleeping for much of it. But we hadn't grown a lot of fat during the 1936 tour, so in no time at all I was knocking on the door of C.J.'s flat in Park Lane.

Amongst his many aviation activities, C.J. was aeronautical adviser to Herbert Wilcox Film Productions at Pinewood and often flew stunts and camera-kites for them himself.

'They want a jumper,' he told me.

'Great!' said I. 'Should be good for ten quid a jump.'

'Ten? Ridiculous! You'll get £50 a jump, and £6 a day for standing by.'

I realized that I was about to enter a different world …

*

We were to do some shots for a film called *Splinters in the Air*, which was one of a popular comedy series. I was glad it was a comedy, for from the little I had heard of jumping for the film industry, that was usually how it turned out anyway.

Benno de Greeuw, who had jumped for MGM, told the story of a job he did with Naomi Heron-Maxwell. The shot that was required was of eight parachutists dropping from a Vickers Virginia above a solid cloud-layer, then disappearing into it. The company couldn't afford eight live parachutists, so they used Benno, Naomi and six reasonably life-like dummies. They flew from Netheravon, to drop over the open spaces of Salisbury Plain. At 8,000 feet they found themselves above decent cloud. The dummies were released from the bomb racks, and Benno and Naomi followed from their cold perches out on the wings. The shot of the eight 'parachutists' disappearing into the clouds was fine, but the villagers of Salisbury Plain who saw the chutes appear from the clouds and come drifting down towards them were understandably intrigued. From a distance, they watched these silent visitors land and saw two of them get to their feet. The others remained lying on the ground, not stirring. They were obviously unconscious. Perhaps dead. What terrible tragedy had befallen these mysterious parachutists? The alarm was all over the county before the 'bodies' were discovered to be rubber dummies.

We also were to use Salisbury Plain for our drops. In an Avro Cadet, accompanied by another kite with the camera crew on board, C.J. and I flew from Heston to a small flying-field at High Post. We intended to film on a Sunday, when there would be no military flying and no firing on the artillery ranges. There was also, at nearby Boscombe Down, a convenient and well-laid-out RAF airfield, an ideal background to one of the shots the director had asked for ...

'I want this shot of the man falling away from the aircraft, and the chute streaming and opening while still in camera range, all against the back-drop of a military aerodrome ... Know what I mean?'

'Dotty' Doig in our 'Flying Flea' in 1936.

Jumping with the Irvin chute, which is just beginning to deploy as I pull the ripcord at something like 500 feet. *Inset*: Dorothy Spicer, fellow jumper Bill Williams and that fine pilot Pauline Gower, with whom I toured in 1936.

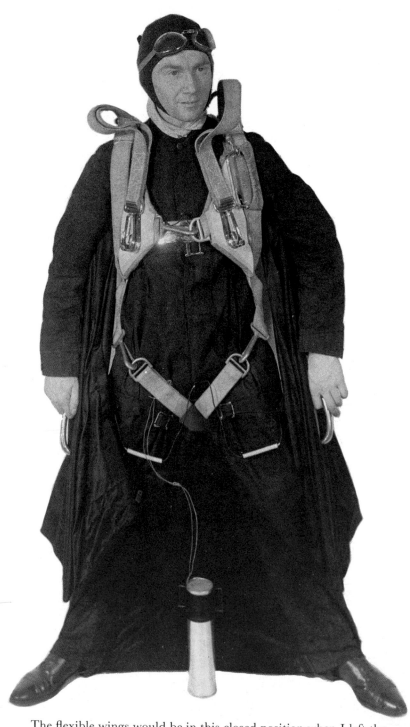

The flexible wings would be in this closed position when I left the
aircraft.

Once in free fall, I would spread the wings into this 'flying' position.

When Cecil Rice built my 'wings' for me, the only way to test them was to have myself suspended from the railway crane at Gargrave Station.

Preparing for a birdman jump during the 1936 season.

Opposite: a Royal Air Force Parachute Jumping Instructor makes descent from the balloon at Tatton Park, with the 'X' typ parachute

Bill Hire, whom I trained as an air circus jumper in 1934, was later to join Bruce Williams and me as PJI with Britain's first paratroopers.

As one of the first Parachute Jumping Instructors of World War Two, I trained many Polish paratroopers, for which I was thanked personally by General Sosabowski.

The officers of the Central Landing establishment at Ringway in August 1940, just before I arrived. The following are notable personalities in the pioneering of parachute training. *Front row*: Jack Benham (third from left), Louis Strange (fourth from left), John Rock (second from right). *Second row*: Bob Fender (second from left), Martin Lindsey (third from left), Boris Romanoff (fourth from left), Mac Monnies (fifth from left). *Back row*: Bruce Williams (fourth from left), Bill Bradish (fifth from right).

Winston Churchill and his entourage watch the troops jump from the Whitley bombers during his visit to Ringway in 1941.

Churchill, accompanied by Group Captain 'Stiffy' Harvey, inspects the paratroops at Ringway in 1941. This visit provided a much needed boost for Britain's young airborne force.

The Whitley, with its dreaded 'hole', was eventually replaced by the side-door Dakota, which proved a much more civilized way of going to war.

Squadron Leader Harry Ward, AFC, RAF.

We planned to take the main shot from an automatic camera mounted on the jump plane, while the camera crew in the other machine would film me actually landing on the airfield.

As a matter of courtesy, C.J. telephoned Boscombe Down to get their approval. He explained who he was and what we were doing, and asked if we might make our parachute descent onto the airfield during the following Sunday morning.

'Certainly not!' was the response.

I knew the airfield at Boscombe Down. I had been there with the travelling demo team in the twenties, and recalled that the airfield was quite a distance from the main camp. I could do the drop and roll my chute, and C.J. could land, pick me up and be away again before anyone could stop us. Neither of us was in the services any longer, so they couldn't have us court-martialled. And if they did kick up a fuss afterwards, well ... the film would already be in the can.

'Let's do it,' we said.

Sunday morning was clear and still. To get that shot of me falling from the plane and of the parachute streaming, an aft-facing camera was positioned on the lower wing of the biplane, alongside the rear outer strut. My part was easy. All I had to do was jump and pull, then land in the middle of that airfield. C.J. had the hard part. He had to hold the kite steady while I was making my way right out onto his wing-tip, then operate the remote-controlled camera and – at the very moment I let go – kick the rudder bar to slew the tail-plane out of the way of that early deployment. The camera had to be angled to take account of all this. We checked it, made sure that it was ready to roll, and climbed into our cockpits.

Timing was going to be critical. I had to arrive on that wing-tip at just the right moment, for C.J. wouldn't be able to hold me there for more than a second or two. That right moment would be when we were in the exact position from which I would fall and drift into the very centre of the airfield. We had to get it right the first time. In order not to alert the enemy, we could make only one pass over the forbidden field. But C.J. always got things right. He was a brilliant pilot.

We lined up a long way out, coming in from the east. As I saw the airfield slide towards us and begin to unroll beneath the rear edge, I clambered out of the cockpit into the prop-blast and began my stroll along the wing, clinging to the bracing wires and making sure to keep my feet on the rear spar: C.J. had enough on his hands without my putting a foot through the fabric. I could sense the strain on him. At last I was standing astride the camera, facing forward into the airflow, just as it had been on the wing of the old Vimy, except that the pay was now a lot better. I reached for the rip-cord, nodded sideways to C.J.'s goggled face, went off backwards and pulled as I saw the tail-plane swing away above my head.

I was using an Irvin for this one, and it banged open and hauled me upright with its usual swift efficiency. I immediately looked down. Perfect! Slap-bang over the airfield, and with hardly any drift to bother with. I slipped to lose height and quicken my descent, and came in for an easy stand-up landing on soft grass. C.J. was only a few seconds behind me, side-slipping the kite into a touch-down just yards away, then taxi-ing in to where I was rapidly rolling up the canopy and lines. With the chute bundled in my arms, I clambered back into the cockpit that I had left only a few minutes earlier. As C.J. swung the Avro into the wind, we saw a couple of RAF policemen running towards us across the grass, waving their arms and signalling us to stop.

'Certainly not!' laughed C.J., as he gave her the throttle and bounced us into the air.

Back at High Post, I repacked the parachute on the floor of the clubhouse, and we were soon ready for the next jump.

Film directors seem to have these bright ideas without giving a lot of thought as to how they are to be transferred onto film:

'We want this shot of a man hanging from a cloud ... Just suspended from the bottom of it ... Know what I mean?'

It is the job of stuntmen not to reason why but to go and

do it, so there we were – C.J., me and the camera crew – standing outside the club-house at High Post scanning the skies above Salisbury Plain for clouds. There weren't any. But it was one of those warm days of rising air when the sky can conjure small puffs of cumulus apparently out of nothing, so we decided to get airborne and wait. Keeping well clear of Boscombe Down, we climbed out over the Tidworth end of Netheravon airfield and milled around, looking for our cloud. Sure enough, I soon saw a beauty beginning to form at about 6,000 feet.

We gave it a few minutes to build, then I signalled the pilot of the camera-plane to position himself below it. He would have to be close enough to get the shot of me emerging from the base of the cloud, but not close enough to chop me to pieces. When he signalled back that he was ready (no radio, of course), C.J. took us up, and as I clambered out of the cockpit and perched myself on the wing-root in readiness, he pointed the Avro at the looming mass of grey. Those were still days when pilots of light aircraft tried to avoid clouds rather than bore straight into them, so for me it was a new sensation to be suddenly hanging there in a swirl of fog at some 7,000 feet. I gave it a couple of seconds, dropped away, gave it a couple more, then pulled. I was still in cloud, swinging there under a canopy that I couldn't see. Very eerie, it was, looking at those liftwebs and rigging-lines disappearing into greyness above my head. It gave me the feeling that I wasn't suspended by anything at all. Then, below my feet, the grey began to turn to yellow, and as I came out of the fog into broad daylight, just for one magical moment it was as though I really was hanging from that small cloud. I was praying that they hadn't missed the shot.

They hadn't. There was the camera-plane banking out to one side of me, the cameraman with one thumb raised. Great!

I was at 5,000 feet, just hanging there under the silk. Salisbury Plain was spread out below me like a slightly hazy map, the little villages tucked into their valleys, and Salisbury itself, with its narrow spire, over there in the distance. Closer were the Army barracks at Tidworth, and

Netheravon, where I had made my first-ever free fall from the Vimy almost ten years earlier. Gradually the horizons rose around me, and the earth came back. It seemed a pleasant enough way to spend a Sunday afternoon.

C.J. picked me up, and we were soon winging our way back to Heston. The other plane had gone ahead with its precious reels of film. We saw the rushes at Pinewood the following morning. They were quite spectacular. The director was well pleased. With £100 in the kitty, so was I.

As it turned out, I made most of my money at Pinewood not from £50 jumps but from the £6-a-day retainer. Cathcart-Jones insisted that I stay at the Pinewood Club, which was attached to the studios and where I would be on call if required. That suited me. The 'club' was a one-time mansion, with an indoor pool, superb accommodation, excellent food and, of course, a much-frequented bar. It had once belonged to Colonel Grant-Mordon who had shot himself after being implicated in the 'Hatry Affair', one of the major financial scandals of the time. Now it provided residence for transient performers. You could bump into all sorts of people in the corridors and restaurant. Anna Neagle, Marlene Dietrich, Noah Beery and Robert Donat were among my fellow residents.

In the room next to mine was the American Arthur Tracey, known as 'the Street Singer'. He had, in fact, been a New York busker, 'discovered' by the film industry and taken off the street to become a star. He used to play his records at full volume and, to make sure that I didn't miss them, would throw open his door and mine and yell, 'Get a load of this, Harry! Get a load of this!'

'Great!' I would shout, just to be polite. 'Great!'

He would dive back into his room and come out again with an armful of the wretched things, yelling, 'Take 'em! Take 'em!'

When I was not required for aerial sequences, I spent my time on the film set and did a few jobs. I even acted the part of a mechanic, dressed for the role and swinging the prop of one of the real Avro Cadets that we had on the set, with C.J. looking suitably daring at the controls.

The male lead for our film was Sidney Howard, who

came from Yeadon. Whenever he saw me on the set, he would greet me in broad Yorkshire, 'How's Bradford, lad?' The leading lady was Helen Pollock. She was playing the part of a French lady – on and off the set. 'My *leeetle* parachuter!' she called me. Richard Hearn, Ralph Reader and Geraldine Hislop were also in the cast. They were a grand bunch. For a mid-morning break the trolley would come down from the commissariat with tea and hot crumpets. We were gathered round the trolley on one occasion when, quite without thinking, I said to the continuity girl, a smashing redhead, 'Your crumpet's a bit singed.' She didn't bat an eyelid, while everyone else roared with laughter.

Our director was Alf Goulding. He was married to a former Ziegfield Follies chorus-girl, a flamboyant lady who used to appear in a coat made of zebra skins. I often sat and chatted with her on the set, and one day she said, 'Harry, you ought to be in the directing business. I'll speak to Alf.'

She spoke to Alf, and Alf offered me a job as a third-assistant-director. From what I had seen of the film business, the prospects for a third-assistant-director were even less certain than those of a professional parachutist, so I said no, thank you very much.

I was at Pinewood for six weeks, picking up my £6-a-day as well as the jump money. It could have lasted longer. I was trying to do a line with the studio hairdresser, a good-looking Scots girl called Maggie. So was the production manager, Tom White. I was well ahead on points. I had taken Maggie out a few times and had visited her at her London flat. Then one morning on the set somebody gave me the nod that Tom White was trying it on with her in one of the dressing-rooms. I barged in and was all set to lay one on him, but he got out just in time. It caused a bit of a rumpus. Maggie went back to Scotland, and Harry Ward went back to Broxbourne, no longer required at the Pinewood Studios.

Although I had blown that one, the film industry had one more go at making a star of me. Shortly after the Pinewood episode I received a call from Denham Studios, asking if I would do a one-jump 'quickie' for a film called *Mister Stringfellow Says No*. I said I would, for £20 plus a flight to Denham and back to Broxbourne. Denham Studios was not in the same league as Pinewood.

'£10,' said the man.

By that time I was experienced enough in negotiating jump fees to recognize a final offer when I heard one, so I accepted, with a suitable show of reluctance. It was still easy money as far as I was concerned.

On the following Saturday morning, an old De Havilland-9 that had seen better days in the First World War picked me up at Broxbourne and flew me down to Denham. I sorted out the details with the camera crews. There would be a camera on the ground, and another in a second machine that would fly alongside the jump plane. Easy.

At a thousand feet I lobbed out of the rear cockpit of the DH-9, gave it a few seconds before pulling the rip-cord and landed right alongside the ground camera. Perfect, I thought. Not so. The airborne operator had muffed his shot and wanted a repeat. He wouldn't get it that day, I told him, and would have to wait until the following Tuesday before I would be free again. It would also cost them another £10 and the same transport arrangements, and what was more, I wanted the full £20 for the two jumps there and then, please. They didn't like that but eventually counted the twenty pound-notes into my hand and flew me back to Broxbourne.

I was back at Denham on the Tuesday. This time, the cameraman – who was no aviator and no great camera-operator either, I believe – flew with me in the DH-9 and started to shoot as soon as I began to climb from the cockpit, to make sure he didn't miss the jump.

I had taken the precaution of asking Roger Frogley to fly down from Broxbourne to pick me up, for I knew damn well that, as soon as the jump was in the can, there would be no return trip for me. It was that kind of a deal.

Mister Stringfellow Says No was an absolute flop. Not surprising, with a name like that. No ... I wasn't cut out to be a film star.

10

Birdman

People who remember the 1930s might recall the name Clem Sohn. He was an American show-jumper, who in 1936 came to Europe with a new idea in parachuting: he would jump with wings attached to his body. However, the reason why people may remember Clem Sohn is not because he jumped with wings but because he died in them in front of 50,000 people and the news cameras. It was a well-worn joke amongst circus jumpers that, if you wanted to make a lasting impression on the public, all you had to do was make a large impression on the ground.

In 1935 Clem Sohn had been just one of many American professional jumpers, touring the show circuit and taking part in the 'spot landing' competitions which had become a feature of aviation meetings in the States. As in Europe, American show-jumpers were always trying to add novelty to their performances, and Clem Sohn hit on a winner. He came up with this idea of jumping with a set of flexible wings, with which he should be able to glide and swoop through the air like a descending bird before he opened his chute. And if he didn't exactly glide and swoop like a bird, well … there wouldn't be anybody up there to see it, would there?

He made himself some wings of canvas, stiffened with light metal rods. He attached them to his arms and to his upper body and made a separate vane to be worn between his legs. When he stretched his arms out and spread his legs, he would resemble a bat in flight. Armed with his canvas wings and a good publicity man, the American birdman made his first appearance at Daytona Beach, Florida. He was a huge success. People flocked in their thousands to see him. Extravagant claims were made about the distances he was able to glide with his wings and, as he had foreseen, nobody was ever close enough to suggest that those claims were perhaps a little exaggerated.

In 1936 Clem Sohn and his publicity man came to Britain, and in early May he began a series of shows that were sponsored and well advertised by the *Daily Express*. When he appeared at Portsmouth, some of our fliers went down to provide a joy-riding service for the crowds. They agreed that the birdman's gliding abilities were being exaggerated by the press reporters, but his act was certainly pulling the crowds in. Wasn't it time, Tom Campbell-Black suggested, that Harry Ward brightened his show with a set of bat-wings?

Well, I was game for anything. We certainly needed something to pull the crowds in, and after all, we couldn't have some Yank stealing all our thunder, could we? My sense of patriotism increased no end when I heard that Clem Sohn was being paid £200 per show.

But where was I going to get a set of wings from? They weren't the sort of things you could buy from Harrods. I contacted Cecil Rice, who had made my caravan for me, and he immediately agreed to have a go at producing some wings. Cecil had an interest in aviation as well as caravans. He made and flew his own gliders, and I sometimes launched him from Middleton Sands near Morecombe, towing him behind a Humber 'touring-car'. When Clem Sohn appeared at a couple of shows in Lancashire, Cecil went to see him, and to have as close a look as he could get at the American's wings.

'He's going to kill himself,' was his immediate forecast.

Clem Sohn was going to kill himself, Cecil Rice thought, because he had no means of jettisoning his wings in an emergency. They were sewn into his suit. If he found that he was unable to control them while he was falling, or if his chute snagged them in any way as it deployed, he would be in deep trouble.

Cecil's prediction almost came true when Clem Sohn jumped at Gatwick on 6 June as part of the show that marked the official opening of the airport. The birdman got into an awful spin and came whirling all the way down to 300 feet before he managed to get his chute open.

Our first design decision, therefore, was that, if I was going to wear wings, I had to be able to dump them quickly if something went wrong. We also thought that I would be able to handle more flying-surface than the American was using. His wings had a span of about six feet. We decided that Cecil should make two sets – one with a nine-foot span, the other of eleven feet.

Back he went to Gargrave, where, with the help of a seamstress and the village bootmaker, he started to put the wings together. He made them of linen with a black satin finish, scalloped at the edges. Each wing had four wooden stiffeners sewn into it, and hand grips on the 'leading edge'. The wings were attached to a stainless steel chest-band by a pair of rat-trap springs which would snatch them back alongside my body and hopefully out of the path of a deploying chute as soon as I released the hand-grips and pulled the rip-cord. There was a locking device to prevent the wings being forced beyond the range of normal shoulder extension and thus tearing my arms out of their sockets. Should I need to jettison the gear completely, that could be done by means of a simple two-pin release system. I thought I would rather be without them in any case once the chute was open, so we added a coiled line so that I would be able to lower them beneath me as I was coming down under the canopy. The most uncomfortable thing about the kit was the stainless steel chest-band, fastened at the back by a pair of wing-nuts. I'd go straight to the bottom if I landed in deep water.

Cecil also made me a jump-suit, very baggy in order to provide even more flying-surface. (Forty years later, and for the very same reason, someone would 'invent' the baggy jump-suit favoured by the young 'skydivers' of the 1970s). He made my suit of the same black material as the wings. If I was going to be a 'bat-man', I might as well *look* liked a bloody bat. A man from Lancashire actually sent us a dead bat, thinking that it might help our design work.

While Cecil was making my wings, I was looking for

another parachute. I needed something with more positive opening characteristics than the Lobe – something with a pilot-chute that would snatch the canopy well clear of the wings when I pulled the cord. Clem Sohn sensibly used an Irvin. By happy co-incidence, while the circus was appearing at Pangbourne at that time, who should call to see me but Soden, my old boss of Northolt days and now commanding a nearby RAF station. He still had one of the original six Irvin trainer-mains that he had brought back from America with him in 1925, and agreed to sell it to me. It must have been the oldest chute in use! I also obtained an observer-type chest-pack with a twenty-four-foot canopy, to use as a reserve. I thought that the circumstances justified such extravagance.

As soon as the wings were ready, I went up to Gargrave to have a look at them. Apart from actually jumping, there was no way of trying them out, of course. The best we could do was to go down to Gargrave railway station and have me hoisted into the air by the large goods-crane. There I was, nicely suspended in a face-down position, wings outstretched, when a passenger train chugged slowly by. The looks on those faces pressed to the windows! News of that soon spread, and I had to repeat the performance at Gargrave station for a couple of reporters from the *Yorkshire Post*. Publicity was a jump ahead of us. It was one of those situations where you become famous for something you haven't yet done. That can be dangerous. You can find yourself in a situation from which you can't easily back out. That's what killed John Tranum. But I had no thoughts of backing out or of being killed, and the publicity was good for trade.

There was just one more problem to resolve before I could actually jump with the wings. The Air Ministry had got to hear about them. What exactly were they, they wanted to know. Was I actually going to *fly* in the things? It would have been poor for the birdman image if I had said no, I wasn't actually going to *fly*, so I said yes, I was. In which case, they said, they would have to be registered as a light aeroplane. I would be happy to do that, I told them. Then was I qualified as a pilot, they wanted to know. I

assured them that I held an A licence and that, as I didn't
intend to carry any passengers, would that do? Yes, they
said, that would do nicely, and did I have any preference
for registration letters? Yes, I said, A-CUNT would do
very nicely. So my wings were registered as a light
aeroplane, and everyone was happy.

Actually, I had no expectations of flying anywhere in
them. I even doubted that I was going to glide very far. We
all knew that the claims made on behalf of Clem Sohn
were over the top. At best I thought that the wings might
help me to get stable during a long drop, that they might
slow my fall a little and that they might give me some light
control over the direction of that fall. The fact is, of
course, that I didn't know *what* was going to happen when
I launched myself into space and spread those wings for
the first time. There was only one way to find out.

When I rejoined the circus with my two sets of wings
and showed them to the flying types, they provoked much
mirth and many a cheery forecast of disaster. When I
suggested to Jimmy King that I ought to make a test drop
over Salisbury Plain, he said, 'No fear! We'll try them out
in public. If you're going to get killed, it might as well be in
front of a good crowd.'

So the first time I jumped with the wings was when Tom
Campbell-Black's Air Display appeared at Stoke-on-Trent
on 15 August 1936. I nearly didn't jump at all, and when I
did, it almost killed me ...

To get a clean departure from the aircraft, I needed a
cabin-plane with a reasonable-sized door, so we had
chartered a DH-Dragon from Renfrew. I planned to use
the nine-foot wings and to jump from 10,000 feet, which
would give me plenty of time to sort the wings out and
hopefully to amuse the crowd with a well-controlled spiral
or two, trailing smoke from the canister attached to the
vane between my legs.

It turned out to be another of those mornings of low
cloud and dismal rain which had plagued our 1936 tour,
but by the afternoon the rain had stopped and the cloud
had lifted to 4,000 feet. I decided to give it a go. If we
could fly above the cloud and perhaps find even a small

gap to give us our bearings, I could drop through it and come flying out of the cloud directly above the spectators, like a true birdman. I was born an optimist ...

We took off, climbed up through the cloud and began to circle above it at 8,000 feet. It was solid. Couldn't see a thing. We milled around for about thirty minutes looking for a break. The pilot was an impatient type and seemed to think that he knew where he was. He levelled the plane up, turned in his seat and yelled over his shoulder, 'We're right over the airfield. Get out!'

I didn't believe him. I could see nothing down there but rolls of dirty grey cloud. I shook my head. 'Go down!' I shouted back.

He spiralled the kite straight down. When we came out of the clag at 4,000 feet, the airfield wasn't in sight. Nor was Stoke-on-Trent. Nothing but brown, boggy moorland, with rocky valleys and a few sheep. We were slap over the middle of the Peak District.

The pilot eventually found his way back to the field. The crowd had been waiting for the highly publicized birdman for over an hour by then, so I had to jump, even though we could get no more than 4,000 feet of clear air. It isn't height that kills parachutists: it's lack of it. And this was almost one of those occasions. I eyeballed the field from the open door of the Dragon as we ran over it, reached one foot out into the slipstream and onto the wing step and dived head first from the plane. Next thing I knew I was on my back, slightly head down, and falling fast. As for the wings, it was like fighting a tent in a hurricane. The airflow was keeping them closed in front of my body, and I was unable to force them open. Then I began to spin. I was acutely aware that time and height were passing, but I couldn't risk an opening in that position. Even the Irvin wouldn't be able to cope with a back-down spin. I managed to drag one of the wings towards my body, and that did the trick. I was immediately flipped over so that I was face-down to the ground, and as soon as I saw that pattern of streets and roof-tops appear below me, I grabbed the cord and pulled. The chute opened cleanly, and with only a few hundred feet to spare.

I drifted in over the edge of the housing estate onto the field. When I landed, still wearing my wings, I didn't get up straight away but just lay there on the grass for a while. The crowd were tickled pink. They thought I'd bought it.

The next day, the circus moved on to Ashton-in-Mackerfield, to perform at Haydock Park. The skies were clear, so I decided to have another go with the wings, this time the eleven-foot pair. They also had curved wingtips, and when I had them fitted, they were so long that I couldn't stand up with my arms by my sides, and certainly wouldn't be able to make a normal exit from the door of the Dragon. We had foreseen this problem. Cecil had made a six-foot-long board with a cellulose surface and a cross-piece at one end to hold it inside the door of the aircraft when it was tilted. Have you got the picture? If not, imagine a funeral at sea ...

When Bill Hire had tightened my wing-nuts and helped me to fix the wings on, I was laid face down on the board, arms and wings by my sides, then carried into the plane as though I was on a stretcher.

'You look bloody ridiculous,' said Bill. He thought it was a crazy stunt, but he hadn't tried to dissuade me, because he knew that, if I got rubbed out, he would become senior parachutist.

They laid me across the fuselage with my head poking out of the open door, which, I can tell you, is a damn' uncomfortable way to travel. I would have felt even more uncomfortable had they told me that, as they were loading me onto the kite, the right wingtip had caught the edge of the door and had snapped. They decided it would be better for my peace of mind if I didn't know about that. Even if I had known, I would still have jumped. Well, not exactly 'jumped' ... I was going to be tipped out like a corpse.

With me on my plank, we flew up to 11,000 feet, which is a cold place to be with your head stuck outside the door. I was anxious to be gone, and as we straightened up and started the run over the field, I operated the smoke bomb a little too early, and immediately filled the cabin with thick clouds of stanic chloride. My despatchers didn't wait any longer. Choking and spluttering, they grabbed the end of the plank, tilted it and sent me slithering head-first into space.

I went out like a bullet. While I was still face down and before the speed of my fall began to build, I spread the wings to catch the air flow. They certainly had a braking effect: nearly tore my arms off. But I was able to hold them and felt one short-lived moment of elation before the right wing suddenly started to flap violently. I twisted my head sideways and could see that the tip was broken and was now streaming and fluttering in the rush of air. I felt myself tilting and turning. As I fought for control, one of my gloves came off, and my lasting recollection of that jump is watching it floating up and away from me like something in a dream. As the speed of my fall increased, I completely lost control of the damaged wing and found myself being flung all over the sky. Seeing no immediate future in the birdman trade, I let go of the wings altogether and yanked the rip-cord.

Again the Irvin did its job, and there I was, hanging under my canopy at some 8,000 feet. Now I was in danger of choking to death. Whilst I had been falling, the smoke from the canister had been whipped away by the airflow, but now it was billowing out from right between my feet, and there was no way I could escape it. I couldn't breathe and I couldn't see, until at last it burned itself out. I was not a happy parachutist.

The crowd weren't very happy either. They had come to see a birdman swooping out of the sky on outspread wings, and all they had been treated to was a puff of smoke almost out of view, and the sight of a quite ordinary-looking parachutist drifting down to land a couple of fields away. However, our commentator had realized that something was amiss and had spun them some story of narrow escape from complete disaster, so they gave me a fair round of applause when I got back to the airfield. They like a tryer, the British public.

I wasn't too disheartened. Parachuting in those days was altogether a process of trial and error. You tried something out, and if it didn't work, you changed what needed changing and went up and had another go. I was confident that most of the problems were now behind me and that, if I got enough altitude and didn't do anything daft, like breaking wing-tips before I even left the aircraft, I would be able to control the wings and give a true birdman performance. It was time to ask Barker what he thought it was worth.

'Ten per cent of the gate money,' he said.

That, I thought, was remarkably generous, particularly coming from Barker. I had expected to negotiate a set rate for each birdman jump. Nothing extravagant, like Clem Sohn's £200. I would have settled for fifty. But ten per cent of the gate? They had flocked in their thousands to see the American, and although our circus audiences were usually smaller than that, perhaps the birdman act would bring the numbers up. That, after all, was the whole idea of it. Ten per cent of the gate sounded even better than my £50, so I quickly agreed, lest Barker change his mind.

So I mended the wings and waited for some decent weather. It was a long time coming. For the shows where I thought we could attract a good crowd, we advertised the birdman act in the local newspapers and distributed posters of a black 'batman' silhouette on a yellow background. As a result, large numbers turned up to see the well-publicized stunt at Sherburn, and later at Dyce airport near Aberdeen, but on both occasions low cloud prevented me from jumping. Not until the season was almost over did I get another chance. It was at Perth. Third time lucky, I thought.

We had the Dragon again. I had taken a dislike to stanic chloride after filling my lungs with it over Haydock Park, so had decided not to jump with smoke flares any more, which also pleased the pilot no end. So they loaded me onto my board and shovelled me out of the door at 10,000 feet. As soon as I hit the air, I spread my legs and opened the wings and waited for something awful to happen. It didn't. I was stable. I wasn't flipped onto my back. I wasn't whipped into a crazy spin. I was just lying there, with the earth spread out beneath me. The strain on my arms was terrific but, with elbows slightly bent, I found that I could hold the wings. I felt as though I was balancing precariously on a tall column of air pressure and that one wrong movement would tip me off it. Tentatively I pulled one arm in a little closer and dipped the opposite shoulder, and sure enough – the earth revolved below me and I sensed that I was swinging round in a wide spiral. I brought both arms closer to my sides, which took some of the pressure off them but also tilted me into a head-down attitude. In that position I felt as though I was really motoring across the sky. At no time did I feel that I was actually flying: I was still falling, and at a rare speed, but I felt that I had some degree of control and that I was getting some lateral movement into the fall. It was exhilarating stuff! I thought for a moment of Corporal East. He would have loved this! And Tom Campbell-Black, who had suggested that I become a birdman – he would have been pleased.

I had no stopwatch, no altimeter. Just a good pair of eyes. I watched the ground coming up, and when I judged it to be about 2,000 feet away, I opened the chute. I released the wings and lowered them to hang below me on their suspension rope, and as I swung down towards the field under the Irvin, I tried to assess the number of faces looking up at me. Ten per cent of their gate-money was mine! Must be a few thousand of them, down there. £100 worth, at least. What lovely people ...

I landed a very happy man. I was then made a little happier in the bar of the Perth aero club, whose members gave me a very warm reception. One of them had been a flying officer on the permanent staff of 601 Squadron in my Hendon days.

'Will you no have a drop of the broth?' asked another, and handed me a beaker full of good malt whisky. Then I went to find Barker and to collect my hundred and some pounds.

'Well done, Harry,' he said, and handed me eleven one-pound notes and a few coins. I had that sinking premonition that Barker had done me.

'What's this?' I asked. 'I thought we agreed on ten per cent of the gate!'

'That's right. Ten per cent of the gate. After all the expenses have been deducted, of course. Fuel, wages, hire of the field, advertising ...'

It was no use arguing. There would be something in the small print. Barker would have seen to that. A sadder and wiser parachutist, I went back to the clubhouse for another drop of the broth.

11

The Last Flying Circus

Clem Sohn and I had wings in common, but what he had and what I didn't have was a good publicity agent. That was my fault. Towards the end of my 1934 tour with British Hospitals Air Pageant, Bill Courtney – who put Amy Johnson and Jim Mollinson on the map – had offered to promote me. He asked me if I would make a jump at the official opening of the Maylands Corner airfield in East London.

'How much?' I had asked him.

'No cash,' he said, 'but I'll set you up with bags of publicity.'

'You can't eat publicity,' I told him, and so lost the backing of aviation's greatest PR man of the age.

So it was that my birdman jumps attracted little more than local interest, whereas when Clem Sohn came to Europe again early in the 1937 season, he was once more preceded by some effective ballyhoo.

After a few shows in Britain, he crossed the Channel to begin a French tour. His first show was at Villacoubly, near Paris. Some 50,000 paid to watch him, and about the same number gathered round the edges of the airfield, for when a man jumps from two miles high, you can see it almost as well from one side of a fence as the other. But on this occasion it was the paying customers who saw the real drama. The American went out at 10,000 and spread his wings. His smoke trail showed that he was getting some lateral movement as he fell, but nothing spectacular. The spectacle came when he pulled the rip-cord of his main chute at about a thousand feet, directly above the centre of the field. The white silk streamed but didn't open. Clem Sohn carried a reserve parachute on his chest. He had the quick reactions of a good pro and wasted no time in whipping out the second rip-cord. But the reserve canopy didn't open either. It snaked upwards and twined itself round the streaming main, and Clem Sohn hit the ground at something like 100 mph. There were reports that the main canopy had caught the left wing as it came out of the pack, and I can believe that. Cecil Rice had been right.

His death brought Clem Sohn the biggest headlines of his brief career as a birdman. That's show-jumping. Although my own 1937 season had begun, it seemed a pity to let all that publicity go to waste. I contacted the organizers of Clem Sohn's French tour, told them of my own experience with wings and offered to complete the American's programme of shows. No, thank you, they said: one dead birdman was enough. So, for me, it was on with the daily and weekly and monthly routine of another British tour, making an occasional jump with the wings, but most of them without.

When Tom Campbell-Black died, King and Barker had sought a new name for their flying circus. For 1937 they had called it 'The Aircraft Demonstration Company'. Not a very dashing name – but then the air circus was no longer a very dashing thing. It was, in fact, on its last legs. We didn't like to admit it, but I think we all knew in our hearts that the end of the era was in sight.

For six years the circuses had been touring Britain. We had saturated the country with joy-riding and air shows. We were also facing impressive competition, not from other circuses but from the main body of military and civil aviation. In 1935 it had been decided to celebrate Empire Day in May with a series of flying displays throughout the country. It had become an annual event, known as 'Empire Air Day', and in 1937 fifty-three RAF stations and civil airports had staged their own shows. Then there was still the traditional RAF Display at Hendon, which that summer staged a fly-past by a mass formation of 260 aeroplanes in five columns. That made our one out-of-date airliner and handful of light aircraft look pretty sick. Nor could we match Hendon's parachute display, in which a scarlet-painted Vickers Virginia was 'attacked' by a flight of the new Gladiator fighters, until smoke was pouring from the bomber and four men bailed out of it in realistic simulation of the real thing.

Also, flying was losing much of the romance and sense of adventure that had accompanied it into the early 1930s. Long-distance racing and record-breaking solo flights no longer stirred the imagination as once they had. That 1936 race to Johannesburg, for which Tom Campbell-Black had been preparing when he died, had been a fiasco and a tragedy. C.W.A. Scott won it because his was the only plane to finish. Other fliers were scattered down the route, several of them dead. In 1937 record-breakers who would once have attracted headlines drew scarcely a mention. Who has ever heard of H.L. Brook who beat Amy Johnson's Cape Town to London record by a full sixteen hours?

No, it all seemed to be going sour in 1937. It was the year the *Hindenburg* went up in flames, to end the age of the airship. It was the year in which 'Captain' Percival Phillips, who had begun barnstorming in the twenties with his Cornwall Aviation Company and must have carried more joy-riders in his red Avro 504 than any other pilot, crashed and died on take-off in a Cambridgeshire field. It was the year in which bombers of the German 'Condor Legion' gave a taste of things to come when they obliterated the Spanish town of Guernica. It was the year in which the dear old Duchess of Bedford got fed up with it all and pointed her Puss Moth out over the North Sea and never came back. It was the last year of the British air circus ...

We began the tour with much the same old crew, except that we no longer had Pauline Gower and Dorothy Spicer with us. Right from the start of our season, attendances were even lower than they had been in 1936. I did some more jumps with the wings, and the advance publicity that we gave those shows certainly pulled a few more people in. They also added to the number of spectators who didn't come in but watched for free from outside the field. We could see them all parked by the roads and picnicking in the nearby fields as we flew and jumped for the ones who had paid.

Because I hadn't been able to persuade Barker to change my 'ten per cent' contract to a fixed fee for each birdman show, I confined my use of the wings to the larger events. I knew that every time I wore those wings I was strapping on a bundle of extra risks, and I wasn't prepared to do that for peanuts. I wore them at Sheffield, where I was tipped out of the Airspeed Ferry at 6,000 feet well upwind of the field and was able to 'glide' back to a good opening-point just inside the boundary. There was another good one over the Wirrall. In fact, although I didn't always get them to do exactly what I wanted, none of my wing jumps during the 1937 tour was as hairy as those first two I had made in 1936. Usually I was able to fall stable and to achieve some measure of control.

The birdman act was a good gimmick and in better times would have been a hit. In better times, I also think that Barker would have wanted me to perform more often with the wings and would have paid a set rate, but in 1937 he just didn't have the money in his pocket, so mostly I jumped without them, and that seemed a bit tame now.

The crowds were definitely dwindling. It was no great fun performing in front of some of the meagre audiences we had. Instead of people queuing up for rides in the Avros, we sometimes had Avros queuing up for people. I had always tried to assume a rather grim expression when landing in front of spectators, just to keep up the illusion that this parachuting lark was a dangerous and fearful business. On the 1937 tour I didn't have to *pretend* to look frightened: I *was* frightened. Frightened I wasn't going to get paid.

Jimmy King doled out what he could, but our arrears of pay mounted steadily. Never mind, we kidded ourselves, things would get better. They didn't. From the first thirty-two towns we visited, the circus averaged a daily income of £89. Before we were half way through, Bill Hire left us. There wasn't enough trade for three parachutists, and certainly not enough cash to pay their wages, so when Bill had an opportunity to move into dance-promotion (booking halls and hiring top-flight bands to play in them), he was happy enough to go. He reckoned he would find even more birds in that profession.

Bill reminds me of that story of the American barnstormer who returned to the scene of a previous year's romance to find that the young lady in question had borne him a son. 'Gee, why didn't you tell me, honey? I'd have come back and married you,' he said. 'Well,' replied the young lady, 'Pa said he'd rather have a bastard in the family than a barnstormer.'

When we said goodbye to Bill, little did we realize that he, Bruce Williams and I would be parachuting together again in very different circumstances some four years later. The man responsible for bringing us together would be Louis Strange, and by coincidence Bill and I met him for the first time that summer when we did a double jump at Ramsgate. Louis Strange had been a fighter pilot in the First World War, in the rank of lieutenant-colonel. He was another of those fliers who felt lost outside a cockpit and had managed to remain in aviation in various capacities. When we met him at Ramsgate, he was managing the aviation holdings of the American millionaire Whitney-Straight.

After those first thirty-two British towns, we crossed to Ireland, and for a while it looked as though things were picking up. The crowds seemed larger. More likely it was an illusion created by smaller fields, for when it was all totted up after our eight Irish shows, the average take was again only £119. But we had always enjoyed our visits to Ireland, and we made the most of this one, perhaps knowing that it would be the last. The gypsies seemed to have got the message too, for there weren't so many of them following the circus with their gambling stalls. But Mrs Lawlors was catering for us once again, and that made up for just about everything.

The Irish tour opened at Phoenix Park, where I made a good jump with the wings, slap over the middle of the show ground and perfectly visible to the fair-sized crowd as I spiralled down from 5,000 feet. Although I didn't know it at the time, that was the last jump I was ever to make with the wings. Ironically, it was a simple jump without the wings that was almost the last thing I *ever* did ...

We were at Greystones, on the coast of County Wicklow.

The attendance was small. There were more people watching from the adjacent beach than there were on the show ground. Trade was so poor that we decided to cut the display short and head off for a night in Dublin.

'Come on, Harry! Quick lob to close the show, then we'll be off,' someone said.

I should have sent up one of those small hydrogen balloons to test the speed and direction of the wind, for we were close to the sea, where an on-shore breeze can change to an off-shore breeze before you know it. But there didn't seem to be much of a breeze from anywhere, and to have messed about with the balloon would have wasted good drinking time, so I strapped on the chute and hurried out to where Jerry Chambers already had the Avro running. Up we went, and out I dived at a thousand feet over what I thought would be the ideal upwind release point. I ripped after three seconds and was tucking the rip-cord handle away inside my overalls when I realized to my horror that, instead of being drifted towards the field and the waiting crowd, I was being blown backwards at a fair rate of knots, over the beach and towards the sea. Too late, I realized that I had been fooled by a deceptive calm at ground-level, caused partly by the line of trees that ran the length of the field on what had become its upwind edge. Now I was about to pay the penalty for utter carelessness.

I looked over my shoulder at all that white-capped wet stuff. I hate water. Never was much of a swimmer. I grabbed handfuls of rigging-lines and slipped the chute like mad, but although I was able to lose height, I couldn't hold the drift. Nor did I have one of the new quick-release harnesses which Irvin had introduced in the early thirties. I had never seen the need to spend hard cash on such a luxury, and still used one of the old three-buckle jobs. Trouble was that you couldn't undo those buckles whilst you were under the canopy, because all your weight was bearing on them.

The folk on the beach, of course, were loving it – and they hadn't even paid to watch me. They were waving to me as I went flying seawards over their heads. They probably thought I was doing it on purpose. I yelled at them in an attempt to persuade them otherwise and to let them know that I was going to need their help, for I didn't see a bright future ahead. They kept on waving.

I had slipped away as much height as I could, and was only a hundred yards out from the beach. It looked like a mile. Then the water came lapping up at me, all greeny-grey, and in I went. As it closed over my head, I was already yanking at the buckles, but by the time I surfaced I was tangled in rigging-lines and wet silk and taking in mouthfuls of salt water. I had the buckles undone and was trying to fight my way out of the harness and the lines. It was like fighting with an octopus, and the octopus was winning. I thought I was a goner. Strangely enough, I didn't seem to mind. It was all quite peaceful. Salt water doesn't taste all that bad when you get used to it. My sight was the first thing to go. I was dimly aware of a familiar voice shouting at me. Bruce Williams ... Good old Bruce ... He seemed to be getting all tangled up in the lines as well. If he was trying to rescue me, I thought, he was making a right cock-up of it. Bert Twyning was there too. It didn't make any difference ... I was under, and quite resigned to it ... it didn't seem to hurt, this drowning business ...

I was vaguely aware of lying face down on wet sand, with someone leaning over me, saying in a lovely Irish accent, 'This one's had it ...'

I wanted to say, 'No, I bloody haven't,' but I couldn't even raise a croak, and drifted away again.

They had tried to pump the sea water from my lungs, but without success. Now they bundled me into a car and, with a doctor and a priest in close attendance, hurried me off towards the local hotel. I was lying across Robbie's lap, apparently beyond help. However, the bumpy track across the beach now succeeded where artificial respiration had failed, for suddenly, all over the flannel trousers of Richmond Fotheringay Robinson, I spewed a fair quantity of Irish Sea and the several pints of Guiness that I had consumed at lunchtime.

It had been a close thing. Afterwards, I discovered how Bruce Williams and Bert Twyning had come haring across the beach from the field as soon as they had seen me heading for the briny. They had swum to where I was threshing about, and although they had got themselves mixed up in the lines and were in no great shape themselves, they had managed to keep my head at least partly above water until someone had organized a human chain to drag us all out.

I was left in the hotel, still in a bad way, but I knew I was going to be OK when the priest stopped looking in on me. After a week in bed, I was able to take a bus from Dublin to catch up with the circus at Limerick. It was in its last throes. There was no money in the kitty and very little coming in through the gate and from the joy-rides. Those who were contracted to Barker and King were pulling out. Our fleet of Chevrolets had already been seized, after the Phoenix Park show. Jimmy King and Barker were both back in Britain, presumably trying to raise more cash to keep us afloat. They failed.

I did a couple more jumps, but as I swung down out of the sky I could almost count the spectators before I reached the ground. At Bundorran we gave our last show. There was no grand announcement. The Aircraft Demonstration Company just ground to a halt as those who had wings or wheels headed back for Britain while they had enough fuel to get them there. It didn't really *end*: it just petered out and left those of us still there scratching our heads and wondering what to do next.

The day of the flying circus was over, and although we didn't know it at the time, it would never return.

I hid the money I had saved, declared myself insolvent like the rest of the crew and was sent back across the Irish Sea under some diplomatic arrangement for the repatriation of 'distressed theatrical persons'.

When Barker and King appeared before the Official Receiver later that year, their Aircraft Demonstration Company had liabilities of nearly £6,000 and assets of one aircraft valued at £177, with 10 shillings cash-in-hand.

We should have seen it coming long before we did, I suppose. The writing had long been on the wall, in pretty big letters, but we had lived in that cheerful mood of optimism that believes in today and lets tomorrow look after itself. We had all hoped that 'tomorrow' would bring a change in fortune, without really seeing any reason why it should. Nor, in June 1937, did we see the demise of the British air circus as an event of any significance other than to ourselves. We were not struck with great sadness at the passing of an era: merely at the distasteful prospect of actually having to work for a living.

There was nothing else in parachuting for me. I knew that and didn't even look. I stowed away my wings and my two Russell Lobe parachutes and the 1925 Irvin and took a job as a mechanic with Imperial Airways, working at Croydon. I missed the excitement. I missed the crowds. I missed the comradeship of the circus crew. I missed the good feeling of doing something that few others do or would even dare to do. I was still involved in aviation, but in a lowly capacity and with a completely different set of characters. Some of our younger mechanics were members of Oswald Mosley's 'Black Shirts'. They had no strong political beliefs: they just went along for the punch-ups. If I had been bigger, I think I might have gone along with them.

I was on the night shift at Croydon, servicing De Havilland Rapides after their day's flying. We worked next door to Lufthansa, a very smart outfit, run on strict military lines. I liked the look of the Junkers-52 three-engined monoplane that used to fly in at night with freight. It would make a nice jump plane, I thought – without realizing that very soon that would indeed become one of its major roles in Hitler's Luftwaffe. At Croydon it was piloted by a type who had flown Zeppelins in the First World War and still wore his old airship overalls.

By 1938, although nobody really wanted to believe it, all the signs were that Europe was drifting towards war. At last, the RAF was being rapidly expanded in long-overdue attempts to match the now-apparent strength of its likely foe – Germany. The old Zeppelin man shook his head sadly, for he knew that his Junkers would soon be putting on its war-paint.

The RAF was advertising for technical instructors for its

new training school at Cosford. I applied and was called to RAF West Drayton for a trade test. My examiner was the same Flight-Lieutenant Gliddon who had been on the training staff at Manston in 1921. Having taught me the business, he could hardly do anything else now but pass me as an instructor. At Cosford, I found that my boss was yet another officer from my Manston days – Flight-Lieutenant Davis.

So, ten years after leaving the RAF, I was back again – not yet in uniform but as a civilian instructor, training apprentices at RAF Cosford. There came that day in the late summer of 1939 when the station commander, Group-Captain Guilfoyle, called us together in the station cinema. The black patch that he wore over one eye made him appear particularly sombre as he announced, 'Gentlemen ... War is imminent ...'

Paratroop Pioneers

Immediately after Group-Captain Guilfoyle had announced the imminence of war, I slapped in two applications. One was for a commission in the RAF, the other for a flying job with the Air Transport Auxiliary. Somehow, I was going to get into the air.

The ATA was the first to react. I was invited to White Waltham, where I took a flying test in a Tiger Moth. 'We'll let you know,' they said. Before they could let me know, I was summoned before a Royal Air Force officer-selection board at Adastral House in Holborn. They must have been hard up, for I was accepted and sent to see a group-captain who would decide what I was to be accepted as. He examined my flying log-books and didn't seem to like the look of them. 'You've done more parachuting than flying,' he said. He shared that innate suspicion that many fliers of aeroplanes have towards those with a preference for jumping out of them, and obviously didn't think I was to be entrusted with a real aircraft.

'Link trainer for you,' I was told.

The Link trainer was the fore-runner of today's flight simulator, and I was to be a Link instructor. It seemed that, for the time being, that was as close as I was going to get to actually flying, but it was a step in the right direction.

I went first of all to Loughborough to become an officer. Who should be the CO there but a certain Wing-Commander Sherrif who had been an officer at Uxbridge when I first joined in 1921! I didn't remind him. At Loughborough, we were taught how to use a knife and fork; how to distinguish rank; how to shout at lesser mortals on the parade ground – which was a pleasant change for me; and how not to consort with the female domestics – which was an unpleasant change.

I went back to London to do my training as a Link instructor, travelling in each day from dear old Northolt, which I found not greatly changed, although the sheep had gone. During this training, I heard that I had been accepted by the Air Transport Auxiliary. Too late. If they had got their finger out a bit quicker, my life would have taken a very different turn.

When qualified on the Link, I was posted to a Coastal Command unit at Silloth, on the Cumberland coast. Neither the place nor the job was very exciting. The Link trainer was basic but surprisingly effective. We had an airman whose job was to keep the place clean, and we used to let him have a go at the controls when things were quiet. One day, J.J. Moll, the KLM pilot who had flown to second place in the MacRobertson race in 1934, took the lad up in an Anson, and the kid flew it beautifully.

We livened the training sessions with the usual tricks, such as turning on the 'rough air' when the pupil was trying to keep a steady course or setting fire to paper beneath the machine and yelling 'Bail out!', but it was mostly pretty dull stuff.

There wasn't much to enliven our off-duty time, either. I had a chance and happy meeting with my old flying-circus chum Richmond Fotheringay Robinson in a pub in Carlisle, but apart from that the highlight of my social life was when I tripped over the dress of the CO's wife while we were dancing and fell onto the floor on top of her. 'Can't you wait, Harry?' came the inevitable cry.

In early August 1940 I had to go down to the Air Ministry, and while I was there I popped in to see my old flying-mentor, Leslie Hollinghurst. We chatted a bit about Northolt days and my years with the circuses, and he suddenly said, 'There's something right up your street. They're starting a parachute school at Manchester. A chap named Louis Strange is running it ...'

It took a few weeks for the necessary strings to be pulled, but in October I was posted from Coastal Command to Ringway as one of the new band of Parachute Jumping

Instructors under Louis Strange.

In an office that looked out over the civil airport at Ringway, Louis Strange told me what had been happening. It appeared that Winston Churchill had been so impressed by the Germans' use of airborne forces in their devastating assault on Belgium and the Netherlands in May that he had issued a directive to the Chiefs of Staff saying, 'We ought to have a corps of at least 5,000 parachute troops.' At a time when we had just come reeling out of Dunkirk and were bracing for invasion, the War Office was not too keen on the idea of diverting resources to what many thought of as a pretty crack-brained idea. However, Winston had spoken, and Louis Strange had found himself at Ringway with an equally bemused major of the Royal Engineers, John Rock, with a directive to set up a parachute training school.

Neither of them had much idea about paratroops, and nor had anyone else. The British military hierarchy had completely dismissed the concept when the Soviets had first demonstrated airborne delivery in the mid thirties. The Air Ministry was particularly reluctant to get involved. It had no suitable transport aircraft, didn't want to divert bombers from their primary task and had never got on with the brown jobs* anyway. Begrudgingly, it sent three old Mark-5 Whitley bombers to Ringway and agreed to provide a maximum of eight instructors. Instructors? The nearest thing the RAF had to parachute instructors were the fabric-workers and parachute-packers from Henlow, the successors to the likes of 'Brainy' Dobbs and Corporal East and myself. Louis Strange had managed to get five of them under Flight-Sergeant Brereton, and the Army had provided six men from their Physical Training Corps who knew even less about parachuting than the RAF types. Fortunately for the immediate future of British parachute training, he had also managed to get hold of Bruce Williams!

Bruce had joined up in 1939, had been trained as

---

* 'Brown jobs' was the RAF's affectionate term for army personnel. Similarly, the RAF boys were known as 'blue jobs'.

air-gunner, had been shot down in a Defiant over the Channel in early 1940 and had come out of hospital just in time for Louis Strange to pick him up for the Ringway job. Small world!

While my posting was being arranged, Bruce Williams had gone in search of Bill Hire. He found him running a London dance-hall, a number which Bill was rather loath to give up, even for a direct commission into the RAF. Bruce told him that, if he didn't take it, he'd probably finish up in an Army cookhouse when his call-up came through, and that appealed to Bill even less, so he joined us. There we were, the three circus pros, all set to teach the British Army to become parachutists. Moreover, who should be in command of the three Whitleys but Flight-Lieutenant Earl B. Fielden, with whom I had shared four happy circus tours when he was piloting the old Argosy!

But this was a very different circus in which we now found ourselves performing. Bruce, Bill and I may have been experienced show-jumpers, but the delivery of troops to battle by parachute was a completely new kettle of fish. Everybody, including ourselves, was starting from scratch. No suitable transport aircraft; no parachute designed for airborne delivery; no training system; no previous knowledge of airborne practice and theory. Just a band of Army PTIs, RAF parachute workers, three ex-circus pros and three clapped-out Whitley bombers under the command of a former circus pilot – that was how the training of Britain's airborne forces began.

There was a glider unit at Ringway, too, and that wasn't any better off. It had a few sporting gliders and several chaps who had flown them for fun before the war and who were now laying the foundations of the huge glider fleets that would eventually carry men into Sicily, Normandy, Arnhem and Germany itself ...

Parachuting had begun before I joined the staff. The first jumps onto nearby Tatton Park had been made on 13 July, with Irvin trainer-mains, used in the old pull-off style from a platform created at the rear of the Whitley fuselage by the removal of the gun turret. It had served as a useful introduction for those who had never parachuted before, but was no way to go to war. For paratroops to be effective on the ground, they would have to be concentrated in space and time, not scattered one by one over the countryside. So the retractable gun turret was removed from the fuselage of the Whitley to create a convenient hole in the floor through which a number of men might drop in sequence. Not – it was sensibly decided – with a manually operated chute. Some form of static-line operation was required so that the chute would be opened automatically as the jumper fell away. Initially, this was achieved by attaching one end of a length of webbing (known as a strop) to the rip-cord handle, and the other to an overhead cable in the fuselage. Fine. Until the cable pulled away from the fittings and the whole lot went in, fortunately on a sortie when dummy rather than live bodies were being used. Strops attached to individual strong-points were then introduced.

It was the old game of trial and error. Try it. If it doesn't work, fix it and try another way. It can be a costly process. The first to pay the ultimate price had been young Driver Evans. He died on 25 July, with his canopy and rigging-lines tangled and streaming above him. There was no reserve parachute, nor would there be for many years to come. Training was stopped while Gregory and Quilter, who had done previous work on statichutes, were brought in to advise. They replaced the manually operated pack with a 'bag' system, whereby the lines and then the canopy were pulled out of a back-pack under tension as the jumper fell away, leaving the 'bag' attached to the static line and aircraft. The system wasn't perfect, but it was a damn sight better than the one that had killed Driver Evans.

They called the new parachute 'the X type', and while it was being tested with dummy loads, one of them became hung up on the tail wheel of the Whitley, almost bringing the kite down. That was too much for Major Rock, who was in charge of the Army aspects of the training. He told the War Office exactly what he thought of the Whitley and refused to let any more of his men jump from it. He was

quite right. It *was* an awful plane for parachuting. The
Bombay or even the old Valencia would have been safer
for training, and he was trying to force the Air Ministry's
hand. Meanwhile Louis Strange had put on a chute and,
with four of his RAF instructors, had gone up and lobbed
out of the Whitley, just to show the brown jobs. The War
Office told Rock that the Whitley was the only plane
available, and to get on with it. Full training of the troops
of the newly formed No. 2 Commando recommenced on
14 August and was in full swing when Bill Hire and I
arrived in October.

Louis Strange was a marvellous man to work for. No
time at all for 'bull' and red tape. When they had decided
to jump through the 'hole' in the Whitley instead of being
dragged one at a time from the rear platform, he had gone
straight to Armstrong Whitworth's to arrange for the
modifications to be made to the fuselages of our kites. By
the time the Air Ministry heard of it and complained about
irregular procedures, the hole was already in use. Louis
Strange had come out of the First World War as a much
decorated lieutenant-colonel and joined the Second as a
pilot officer. The Air Ministry could not believe that it was
the same person and listed Louis Strange twice in the Air
Force List. He boasted that he had received two salaries
for almost a year, until the error was discovered. Now a
squadron-leader, he had already received a bar to his DFC
by flying a Hurricane out of France under the noses of the
Germans.

The first thing Louis Strange said to Bill Hire and me
when we reported for duty was, 'Lay off the paperwork.
Come and see me if you've got anything to tell me. I don't
want to be drowned in bumf ...' That suited us fine. We
went off to find a couple of chutes and Earl Fielden's
Whitley, to see for ourselves what this static-line jumping
was all about.

In parachute training today, it is usual for a trainee to
gain confidence from several static-line jumps before
progressing to free fall and manual operation. With me, it
was the opposite. By 1941 I had made almost a couple of
thousand jumps (I never actually counted them), and

every one of them had been with a rip-cord, including those early lift-off descents. I took a dim view of this static-line business. I also liked to pack and to 'unpack' my own chute, not put my welfare into the hands of another parachute-packer and a length of webbing line.

And that Whitley was diabolical! I was used to an open cockpit and diving from the wing into clean, clean air, or perhaps jumping from the pleasant cabin of a Dragon or the old *Spider*. The fuselage of the Whitley was never made for passengers, let alone ones with bulky parachutes on their backs. It was merely a dark, narrow tunnel designed to join the nose to the tail. Into this sewer-like passageway one crawled on hands and knees to take a seat on the cold floor, five men forward of the hole and five aft if there was a full stick of ten jumpers. Being on the forward side was much preferred. From aft, there was a tendency for the legs to be blasted backwards as they entered the slipstream and, as the body pivoted, for the face to be smashed against the forward edge of the hole. 'Ringing the bell' it was called.

Bruce Williams briefed Bill and me on the drill and told us to jump when the red light above the hole went off and the green came on. That was something else I didn't like. I never had been keen on pilots telling me when to leave their aeroplane. We were two uncomfortable and unhappy ex-circus jumpers sitting in that dark, smelly fuselage as it swayed and roared its way to Tatton Park, and were both glad when it was time to get out. Bill went first. When the red light came on, he swung his feet into the hole and sat on the edge. Green on … and he was gone. There was a whoosh of air up through the aperture, and his strop tightened and slapped against the aft edge as I shuffled sideways on my bottom, swung my legs into space, pushed off with both hands, straightened my body and slid into fresh air and sunlight and the slap of the airflow, standing to attention like an 'erk' on parade. What a bloody ridiculous way to leave an aeroplane, I was thinking as I slipped my way down towards the green spaces of Tatton Park for the first time. No wonder the troops didn't like it. No wonder more than thirty of them had refused to jump. No wonder two of them had been killed.

I told Louis Strange what I thought of the Whitley.

'What we need are a few DC-3s,' I said. The DC-3 was a low-winged monoplane with a side door, an ideal plane for parachuting, as subsequent events would show. 'If we can get a fleet of destroyers from the Yanks on "Lend-Lease", surely we could get half a dozen aeroplanes?'

The boss shook his head sadly and explained that it had been difficult enough to get Whitleys. For the time being, we would have to make do with them. I said no more, for if Louis Strange couldn't get better aeroplanes for us, nobody could. Fortunately, most of the troops accepted the failings of the old bombers with the true humour of the British 'Tommy'.

'I suppose the reason they keep their wheels down when they're droppin' is to slow 'em up a bit,' said one to another as they supped their mugs of tea and watched the Whitleys running in to spill another load over Tatton Park.

'Nah,' said the other. 'They keep the wheels dahn 'cos they can't get 'em up. Rusted solid.'

We had no parachuting gear for those early jumps. No overalls; no helmets; no fancy boots. I always jumped in uniform. I still had an old Sidcot flying-suit that I wore over it in cold weather, and sometimes we jumped in greatcoats, with tails flapping. On our feet we usually wore flying-boots, although they had a tendency to go flying off on their own if the opening shock was a bit heavy. Helmets came later. The original 'helmet' was a simple band of 'sorbo' rubber worn round the forehead, not for protection on landing but against the painful effects of 'ringing the bell' during that dodgy exit from the Whitley. The idea was eventually incorporated in the canvas-and-rubber helmet which PJIs wore right through to the 1960s, although the troops themselves soon adopted their distinctive airborne helmet.

When they had started the Parachute School, Strange and Rock and their mixed band of instructors had been given no time to prepare for their pupils, nor to carry out trials on techniques and training methods. In fact, the trainees had arrived at Ringway before the staff. They were 342 men of B and C Companies of No.2 Commando, and they were keen to go. They had taken part in those early drops and were pioneers in the same sense that their instructors were. Rock and Strange had initially recommended a training programme of eight jumps per man, starting with two pull-off descents, followed by six jumps 'through the hole' at progressively lower altitudes. The last two were to be at 300 feet! Bruce Williams had gently suggested that, for training, 300 feet was a bit low, that the pull-off drops were a waste of time and that eight jumps per man was impracticable and unnecessary. Strange had agreed, and by the time I joined the staff, we were thinking that four jumps from 600 feet would be enough for basic training, after which the troops should progress to dropping of a more operational nature.

We kept the techniques of jumping as simple as possible. We were concerned with getting out of the aircraft safely and with landing in one piece. There wasn't going to be enough time between the two to spend on fancy canopy-control. The getting-out required a drill for approaching the hole as swiftly and as safely as possible, and an exit technique that would give the jumper a reasonable chance of dropping through the dustbin-like aperture without 'ringing the bell'. For landing, we merely taught the parachutist to relax the body as he approached the ground, with head and shoulders forward, legs hanging naturally, knees a little bent, and feet together. They were told to resist all temptation to brace for landing, but instead to fall and roll in the direction of drift. We taught a basic shoulder-roll, but the emphasis was on relaxation. A relaxed body might get bruised but was unlikely to get broken. Later, with more experience, this basic technique would be refined, and parachute flight drills would be added to damp out oscillation and reduce canopy drift. But in 1940 we were just starting – from nothing but our own experience.

To teach those basic requirements, we gave trainees a small amount of ground training, interspersed with those large doses of PT and running that the Army consider essential to man's physical and spiritual welfare. Bruce Williams had an inventive mind, and from very limited resources he provided the apparatus for this ground training: a mock fuselage of a Whitley for practising the aircraft drills and the exit through the hole; suspended harnesses for learning the parachuting position and how to cross the liftwebs to face down the line of drift; and jump-platforms for landing-practice. He also introduced the 'fan' trainer for dropping troops from the rafters on the end of a wire at a reasonable rate of descent. He got the idea from a fire-escape system and initally used sandbags as counterweights. Inevitably, the time came when Bill Hire removed one of the sandbags while Bruce was testing the kit: he come down at an awful lick, cursing all the way. The counterweights were eventually replaced by a pair of fan-blades that provided resistance to the drop by beating against the air. It was a frightening apparatus, and a useful progression towards the even greater challenge of the drop from an aircraft. Later, when more knowledge and funds became available, improvements to the 'synthetic apparatus' would be made, but it was Bruce Williams who introduced much of the kit for which others would one day be given the credit.

It was also Bruce Williams who recommended that we should have a tower, for dropping parachutists under controlled conditions. We had heard of the towers used extensively in the Soviet Union, where jumping had been encouraged as a sport for the masses during the 1930s, and Bruce approached a firm of construction engineers, Redpath & Brown, for an estimate. They came back with a cost of £30,000 for a 350-foot parachute tower. The proposal was put to the War Office. The War Office said no. Jumping from captive balloons as an alternative and cheap means of introducing trainees to parachuting was suggested, and although nobody was very keen on the idea, an order was made for a cage that could be suspended beneath a standard barrage balloon.

When the cage was ready, Warrant Officer Rudland, who was in charge of the Parachute Repair Section at Henlow, lobbed out a few dummies at 250 feet. It took most of those 250 feet for the chutes to open, but deployment was smooth enough, and all seemed set for a live trial. I went down to the Balloon Development Establishment at Cardington, with Captain Elliot representing the Army.

At Cardington, I met old Major Spencer. I had watched him parachuting from balloons at Bradford when I was a lad, and in the 1920s he had made some jumps with Holt's 'Autochute' at Stag Lane, and so had his daughter. His father and uncle, Percival and Stanley, had been amongst the most famous of the aerial showmen of the 1880s and 1890s, and his grandfather had been an eminent balloonist of an even earlier era. 'Spencer' parachutes had been used for bailing out of observation balloons during the First World War, so old Captain Spencer had quite a background and knew what he was talking about when he assured me that the balloon would be an ideal training-vehicle for parachutists. I thought so too. Captain Elliot wasn't so sure. He wore a dubious expression as he watched a rather ancient barrage balloon being towed out of the Cardington airship shed. It was covered with bird muck from a long sojourn in the hangar and looked very droopy. 'Just about stand one lift ...' said Major Spencer.

Attached to the winch, the said balloon was towed to the lee of the hangar, where the open cage was fixed beneath its belly. It wasn't so much a cage as a big hole with a ledge round it. We fitted our X types, loaded a couple of dummies into the cage, took our own places, hooked our static lines and those of the dummies to the strong-points above the hole, checked them, and off we went. It was a lovely sensation. Instead of us going up, it was as though the ground was dropping away. There was absolute silence except for the sound of the winch motor and the cable paying out over the drum.

At 300 feet the balloon halted with a slight jerk, swaying gently at the end of its cable. It was all clear below, so I heaved the first dummy out and watched the canopy stream and open with time to spare. Out went the second, and that too was lowered safely to the deck under a fully opened chute. Our turn next. I yelled down to the winch-operator to give us 500 feet, and off we went again. As we rose above the level of the airship shed, the wind that was rolling over its roof hit us. The balloon began to swoop and swing, and the silence was replaced by the moan of the air through the rigging-wires.

'Great, isn't it!' I said to Elliot. He didn't answer. He was looking decidedly pale.

The cable jerked us to a halt again, but the balloon kept dipping and the cage kept swaying. Five hundred feet.

'I'll go first,' I said, thinking that might cheer him up. It didn't. He was hanging on like grim death and trying not to look down.

I made sure that there was a good angle on the cable, so that we wouldn't fall onto it, checked the attachment of my static line again, said 'Cheerio' to Elliot and dropped through the hole.

When you jump from an aircraft, either in free fall or on a static line, you don't get the feeling of actually dropping – none of that sinking sensation. It is dispersed by the momentum of the aircraft and the throw-forward effect that has on the body. From the balloon, however, it was straight down into still air for almost 200 feet – a lovely sensation! Real fair-ground stuff. Then the ripple of silk going about its business, and the drag on your shoulders putting your stomach back where it belongs, and there is that lovely open canopy smiling down on you! Smashing! We were onto a winner – I knew it straight away. No slipstream to cause malfunctions. Less chance of twisted lines. Less likelihood of bloody noses from 'ringing the bell'. Better observation of pupils' performance. Definitely a winner.

I made an easy stand-up landing close to the winch and looked up for Captain Elliot, ready to dodge in case he was right above me. There was no sign of him. I bundled my chute and looked up again. Still no sign. Probably enjoying the view. I gave him another couple of minutes and was about to tell them to haul the balloon down when his figure came tumbling untidily through the hole, and the chute slapped open above him. He landed in a bit of a heap.

'Wasn't that great!' I said.

'No, it bloody well wasn't!' he replied.

That worried me. If he put in an adverse report, we would never get our balloon. By the time we were back at Ringway, I had persuaded him to submit a report that was generally favourable, although he still insisted that jumping from the balloon was the most terrifying thing he had ever done.

To my surprise, very few people liked the idea of it. Even Bruce Williams was against the balloon and would rather have had his tower. Fortunately, Louis Strange favoured the balloon, and it was eventually agreed that we would be equipped with them some time in 1941. When they eventually arrived, Bruce Williams had the honour of being the first to jump from it at Tatton Park, before an audience of Airborne brass. He hated it. The Army weren't impressed either, and it would take several months of use by the RAF instructors to persuade the brown jobs to include balloon jumps in the training programme.

Another suggestion that I made was that the X type's Irvin canopy should be replaced with something that gave more stable flight – such as the Lobe. Any of our trainees landing on a down-swing under the Irvin was heading for a bad knock. Most of our serious injuries could be traced back to the oscillation of the chute – as poor Major Rock had discoverd when he finished up in hospital with severe concussion in late August. Mindful of Louis Strange's aversion to paperwork, I decided not to write about it but to show what I meant. I still had my two Russell Lobes. Bill Hire and I stuffed them into a couple of X-type bags without bothering to fold or stow the lines, also packed four 'proper' X types, attached dummies to the whole lot and persuaded Sergeant Cutler to drop them from 300 feet right in front of Strange's office. The Russells were open even before the Irvin canopies and came down without a murmur, while the Irvins were swinging all over the shop. Louis Strange was impressed, but all we got for that one was a rocket from on high and a very firm instruction to stop mucking about with unofficial experiments.

Experiments in airborne matters were rightly the business of the Development Unit under Wing-Commander Mungo Buxton, although his work was primarily on gliders. The Development Unit, the Parachute School and a Glider Training Squadron under Squadron-Leader Tim Hervey were the three units of what was called the Central Landing Establishment. Tim Hervey had been Louis Strange's rigger in World War I. Another coincidence was that I had been rigger on 601 Squadron at Hendon to another member of CLE, Wing-Commander Sir Nigel Norman.

That initial batch of trainees at the Parachute School – the men of No.2 Commando – were a hard bunch, but some of them were not hard enough. Although all were volunteers for parachute training, when they came face to face with the reality of it, thirty of those 342 were unable to pitch themselves through that hole in the floor of the Whitley. Not surprising. It was a diabolical system, and the accident rate was high in those early days. Two more men died before the end of 1940, and there were far too many bods limping about on crutches or wearing the battered faces that were the reward for 'ringing the bell'. Yes, it was a hard business, and those types who pioneered it without benefit of previous parachuting experience deserve the highest praise.

In addition to No.2 Commando, before the end of the year we were training an increasing number of special agents. The 'specials' came either singly or in small groups, in all shapes and sizes, and with a bewildering variety of foreign accents. There were hardly any jibbers amongst them. Oh, they were scared of jumping right enough, the same as every other trainee, but somehow they would get themselves through that awful hole. I suppose that they, to a greater extent than most, had already come to terms with death as their likely lot. Brave, brave people.

Despite the dangerous and serious nature of the job – or perhaps because of it, there was plenty of fun to be had at Ringway in those early days. I suppose that we ex-circus types brought a certain irreverence into the military atmosphere. One thing we didn't like was parading.

Wing-Commander Strudwick, who was the station CO, loved it. He insisted that all officers and men should attend a full station parade every Saturday morning. Not if we could help it! Bill Hire and I suddenly discovered a pressing need to carry out a close investigation of the deployment curve of the X-type parachute as used from the Armstrong Whitworth Whitley Mark-5 aeroplane. At least, that's what we told Strudwick. We explained that, much as we would regret having to miss the station parade, the only time we could carry out these trials without disrupting normal training was on Saturday mornings. We had willing allies amongst the crews, so every Saturday Mac Monnies would wind up the Whitley, Bob Fender would fly the Hawker Hind, with Lawrence Wright on the camera, and Bob Hire and I would lob out over Tatton Park, to be collected by jeep and taken to a cosy little café at Knutsford for the rest of the morning.

We had some good parties. At first I was billeted out in digs at Withenshaw, but early in 1941 I took over a cottage that belonged to the entertainer Wilfred Pickles. It was equipped with a beautiful piano, on which Earl B. Fielden entertained us at many a rip-roaring do.

Bill Hire certainly hadn't changed his ways. We were knocking a few back in the Grand Hotel in Manchester one evening when we heard some brash young type bawling out the hall porter, who was a pleasant enough old soldier. When the young fellow came past, Bill tripped him up, then booted him through the potted palms into the orchestra. The chap's companions immediately came for Bill, who took off up the main staircase with half a dozen in pursuit. As he neared the upper floors, a door opened, and Bill darted through, to find himself in the room of a very attractive young lady. Not only was he saved from a thumping: he stayed the night. Such things could only happen to Hollywood heroes and Bill Hire.

In January 1941 a new batch of aircrew arrived at Ringway with their own Whitleys, commanded by Wing-Commander Tait. There was also a stir amongst the troops – no longer called No.2 Commando but renamed 11

Special Air Service Battalion. Something was brewing. Our suspicions were confirmed when Bill Hire, Bruce Williams, Bill Brereton and I found ourselves acting as guinea-pigs for night dropping trials on the airfield. No fun. Night parachuting never is, particularly in January, when the ground is hard and the visibility sometimes doubtful. It was not for our benefit, though, but for that of the navigators and pilots, and as soon as they had sorted out their night dropping procedures, we turned our own attention to training some of the Army boys for what was obviously going to be the first operational drop by British airborne forces. The simmering excitement of 11 SAS had become concentrated on just fifty of them, known as X Troop, under the command of Major T.A.G. Pritchard.

We didn't know where X Troop was going, nor when. We knew that Mac Monnies had made a scale model of the target area in Group-Captain 'Stiffy' Harvey's office, but that was strictly out of bounds to all but a few. All we knew was that we had to get X Troop into top shape for an airborne assault at night. So we drilled them hard in aircraft procedures; in jumping quickly one after the other as a group (known as a 'stick' of jumpers); parachuting at night; and rapid assembly on the ground. There wasn't much we could teach them about landing in the dark: just constant reminders to hold a good position and stay relaxed as they waited for the ground to come up and hit them.

It became apparent that their target was going to be some sort of bridge or aqueduct when a full-scale and closely guarded mock-up appeared at Tatton Park. They were out there every night, banging away at it.

Training with the troop was a quiet and pleasant little Italian, called Picchi, who had been a hotel-worker in London. There was also a strange character called Flying Officer Luckey. Who he was, where he came from, what he did and where he went to when it was all over, nobody knew. He was the only one of the troop and the training team who was allowed off base: the rest of us were confined to camp during the training and rehearsals.

January was not a good time for training paratroops.

The hard grounds took their toll of ankles. Then, on 22 January, Lance-Sergeant Dennis was blown off the dropping-zone to crash through the ice on a nearby pond. He became stuck in the mud and drowned before rescuers could pull him out. Strong winds also threatened the dress-rehearsal on 1 February, and several of the troops were blown into high trees. But they were a gutsy bunch, and nothing could deter them. We shared their delight that at last their parachute training was going to be put to good use. We were very proud of them.

On 7 February the eight Whitleys, their crews and X Troop flew off into the dusk. With them went Wing-Commander Norman, Bruce Williams and the little Italian, Picchi.

The next we heard was from a brief newspaper report on 20 February, telling the world that a small force of British paratroops had been dropped successfully in southern Italy. Only later would we piece together the story of X Troop. They had mounted from Malta in six of the Whitleys. Their target was the Tragino aqueduct in the hills of southern Italy. Five of the aircraft had dropped their men right alongside the objective, but the sixth had put most of the sappers and their explosives into the next valley. The aqueduct was damaged but not destroyed, and X Troop had set off towards the coast to rendezvous with a submarine. None of them made it. All were captured in the barren hills. Picchi was shot.

13

The Muscle Mechanics

Another casualty of Britain's first airborne operation was Bruce Williams. He returned from the raid – on which he had flown in his role as an air-gunner – but once back in Britain he spilled the beans to a reporter, and the story was splashed over the *News of the World*. It was by then no secret. In fact, one of the objectives of the raid had been to announce to the world the existence of a British airborne force, so Bruce had done no great harm. He had, however, broken the rules. He was removed from parachuting duties, charged with disclosure of classified information and court-martialled.

Louis Strange defended him desperately, not wishing to lose the most valuable man on his staff, but to no avail. Bruce had to go. 'You wouldn't think we were fighting a war!' fumed Louis.

Bruce Williams did more than any man – other than Louis Strange himself – to set the training of Britain's paratroopers on the road. He was a great loss to the Parachute School, but his war wasn't over. He trained as a pilot in Canada, flew Lysanders on Special Operations and won the DFC.

While the skids were being put under Bruce Williams, another officer joined us at the school. Charles Agate had been a PT teacher before joining the RAF and being trained as an air-gunner. He had been posted to duties as a ground instructor, which didn't appeal to him any more than being a Link instructor had appealed to me. He had read about the Italian raid and the existence of a Parachute Training School, and applied for a transfer to parachuting duties, which sounded more exciting than gunnery-instruction.

157

When he reported in his best uniform to Louis Strange, the boss chatted to him for a few minutes, then sent him straight to me for training.

'You're in luck,' I said. 'We've got a kite going off for a dropping sortie in a few minutes.'

I had him fitted with an X type and put on board a Whitley, with its engines already running. A few minutes later, over Tatton Park and still wearing his best uniform, he jumped No. 1, ahead of seven Norwegian troops. He had been at Ringway almost an hour. Nothing like the 'deep end' method, I always thought. It certainly worked for Charles Agate, for when he was subsequently established as our resident dropping-zone officer at Tatton Park, he developed an almost unhealthy enthusiasm for jumping from the balloon.

'Operation Colossus', as the Italy raid was called, was a bold venture, but the target was hardly worthy of the bravery of the troops and the skill of the fliers who got them there. The attack did little material damage to the enemy and failed to impress the War Office, who in general continued to see airborne training as an unwelcome diversion of effort and resources. By the end of the winter at Ringway, we were in sore need of a boost. It arrived in a bowler hat and puffing on a cigar on a wet and windy Manchester day in April 1941: Winston Churchill ...

The great man had come to Ringway to see how the 5,000 parachute troops he had asked for were getting on. He saw a force of fewer than 400. Most of them were standing on the parade ground, for the only live drop we could muster for him was a jump by forty men from five ancient Whitleys. The glider boys managed to display five Kirby Kite sport gliders and one of the new Hotspurs, capable of carrying six troops into battle.

After he had watched the jumpers go skittling across the sky like leaves in the wind, he turned and walked away. Louis Strange was at his side. 'Listen, sir, you know nothing about this ...' I heard him say. Then they were out of range, but I could see that Louis was giving the PM a right talking-to. John Rock and Nigel Norman and

Group-Captain 'Stiffey' Harvey also had a go at him, and Churchill made a point of chatting to some of the troops and instructors before he left.

He may have been disappointed by the scale of what he had seen, but the straight talking and enthusiasm of Louis Strange and the others had undoubtedly impressed Churchill, for within a few weeks we heard that there was to be a major increase in the strength of airborne forces. It was the start of an expansion that by 1945 would provide Britain with two airborne divisions.

How things changed after Churchill's visit! Apparently he gave the Chiefs of Staff a bit of a rocket and told them to get their fingers out. He *wanted* those paratroops he had asked for. Suddenly we were no longer the poor relations. Everyone wanted to get on the airborne bandwagon. Sadly, that meant pushing some of the original team off.

Louis Strange himself was the first to go. After less than a year in charge of the Parachute School, he was posted to command the Merchant Shipping Fighter Unit at Speke, training pilots to fly Hurricanes that were catapulted from the decks of merchant vessels at sea. It sounded even more dicey than parachuting. He deserves more credit than he ever got for leading that small band of RAF and Army pioneers who laid the foundations for British Airborne Forces. It would be easy for some of those who came later to smile at the naïvety and some of the inadequacies of the earliest days of airborne training in Britain. They should remember that Louis Strange had *nothing* to build on: they built on *Louis Strange*.

His place was taken by Jack Benham, who had been his second-in-command since almost the beginning and who would have carried on in the same mould had he lived long enough. Jack had taken a particular interest in the training and delivery of 'specials'. He flew on their operational missions whenever he could, partly to learn from experience and partly to give them the comfort of his presence on those terrifying journeys into occupied territory. A fortnight after taking over from Louis Strange, he flew with a small group of Poles to despatch them over Central Europe. The kite and all on board were lost without trace.

The post of CO passed to the school's administrative officer, Maurice Newnham. He had flown in the First World War and, like Louis Strange, had rejoined the RAF for the Second. He would command the Parachute Training School right through the war and would build it into an academy well suited to the airborne brotherhood. He never claimed to be much of a parachutist, but he was an excellent administrator, an ambitious empire-builder, and he got on well with senior brown jobs. He didn't always get on well with junior blue jobs, though. Earl B. Fielden was one of the first to fall out with Newnham and was soon on his way, taking Mac Monnies with him. Another of our Whitley pilots, Boris Romanov, asked to be transferred to operations and was killed on his first sortie.

Army personalities were on the move too. John Rock went and was later to die in a glider crash. Colonel Jackson was soon to be replaced as the CO of 11 SAS, now to become the 1st Parachute Battalion under Colonel Ernest Down, known to all as 'Eric'. He was a harder disciplinarian than Jackson, who had allowed his troops to be billeted out in Knutsford, where they enjoyed a high old time. Down brought them into hutted accommodation, and when he called them together for his opening address, he told them in no uncertain manner that their 'ballet-dancing' days were over. They booed him! But he was soon to earn their respect and to become one of the great airborne commanders of the war. 'Dracula', they called him.

In August we heard that a full brigade of four parachute battalions was to be formed and that the Poles were to have their own airborne force. We had already trained troops of the 1st Polish Rifle Brigade, and in August I flew in an Oxford to their base at Leven, in Scotland, to help them set up their own ground-training facilities and a parachute-packing centre. I took some X types with me, and they used them to give a parachute display for General Sikorski. It was after this jump that Sikorski announced to the paraded troops the formation of a Polish Parachute Brigade, to be commanded by Sosabowski. That called for a celebration. I was invited to join the officers in a local hotel, where the dining-room was prettily laid for afternoon tea. It wasn't tea that we drank from those elegant cups. It was neat vodka.

The training of three more battalions called for a major increase in the capacity of the Parachute Training School. Newnham also wanted to extend the training course, with a more formal period of ground training and additional descents. Bill Hire and I disagreed. Our view was that we were training airborne soldiers, not airborne gymnasts, and that this could be done most economically with a minimum of ground training followed by two jumps from the balloon and three from aircraft. The qualified troops could then do training of a more operational nature, still under the supervision of instructors.

'Ah, but if we have a longer course, we shall need a larger staff, and that could mean promotion for you two,' said Newnham.

'Aye, and for you, too!' said Bill Hire. I believe that our days at the Parachute School were numbered from that time.

Newnham was also keen for the RAF to assume full responsibility for parachute training and to put an end to the bickerings that had sometimes arisen from dual Army/RAF control. Not at instructional level, I hasten to add. Any bickering was above our heads. We just got on with the job. Newnham's solution was to draw all future Parachute Jumping Instructors from the RAF Physical Fitness Branch. This was agreed by all concerned except those of us already on the job, and our opinion wasn't asked. 1 November 1941 was set as the target date for the RAF and its PTIs to take over.

'Bloody muscle mechanics!' said Bill Hire.

The first to arrive was Flight-Lieutenant John Callastius Kilkenny. 'J.C.K.' was a games-player of repute, but with no knowledge of parachuting, and little inclination for it. Newnham told him that his role would be to organize and supervise the ground training, while I looked after the actual parachuting, and on that basis J.C.K. would not have to do much jumping himself. That was not Kilkenny's style. If he was going to teach it, he was going to

do it, so at the earliest opportunity I took him out to
Tatton Park for his first jump, from a balloon. He may
have been a good footballer, but he was a bloody awful
parachutist!

We shared an office, J.C.K. and I, and as fellow
Yorkshiremen we got on well enough. He was soon
covering pages of paper with charts and diagrams and
fancy squiggles which, he explained, were PT symbols. I
told him and taught him what I could, including the basics
of the shoulder roll. I also explained the various pieces of
apparatus that Bruce Williams had devised and which now
would become his responsibility. In fact, the ground-
training hangar would soon become known as 'Kilkenny's
Circus', and the landing-technique as 'Kilkenny's Roll', but
it must be said that J.C.K. never promoted himself in this
respect. It was done for him, mostly by Maurice
Newnham.

Later, in October, the PTIs, personally selected by
Newnham, began to arrive in batches for their two-week
course. They were a good crowd. A few didn't make it
through the course, but those who did were destined to
build a very solid school on the foundations provided by
the first generation of instructors, that mixed bunch of
RAF fabric workers and Army PTIs. The sad thing – and I
never forgave Newnham for it – was that, as soon as the
original instructors had taught the new boys all they knew,
most of them were quietly given the push. The Army PTIs
were withdrawn altogether, and most of the RAF lads
returned to their original trade or volunteered for
training as air-gunners. They had given sterling service
for little reward. They had been fobbed off with the rank
of acting-unpaid-sergeant, were not allowed to wear any
form of airborne wing and had received not an extra
penny of pay for parachuting, flying as despatchers on
training sorties and even flying on operational missions to
chuck out the 'specials' over enemy territory.

You were badly done by, Bill Pacey, Paddy Gavin, Bill
Walton, Kim Campbell, Lofty Humphries, Frankie
Chambers, Jerry Oakes, Taff Roberts, Paddy Wicklow and
young Horwood – but by God, you did a grand job!

As I said, Newnham was no great parachutist, and he broke his leg on one of his early jumps. So did J.C.K., but they were both game enough. From somewhere, Newnham and 'Dracula' Down got the idea that they would like to do a jump from the balloon at night. They also got the idea that I should accompany them. I could see no sense in it and told them so. The only thing you achieve by jumping at night is a greater likelihood of getting hurt. Jump at night when you have to, never when you don't. That was always my policy. But Newnham insisted, so off we went. It wasn't merely dark: there was thick fog, too, and no wind. I had to give the balloon-crew instructions to crawl the winch across the dropping-zone while the balloon was airborne, to ensure that there was an angle on the cable. We jumped, and nobody was hurt, but we spent half an hour looking for each other on the ground. Waste of time. The only good thing about it was the slap-up meal I had on Newnham at Cotton's, near Tatton Park.

Another idea of Newnham's was that we should parachute into Rostherne Mere, which bordered Tatton Park – in December. Parachuting into water, it was thought, would be a good means of delivering 'specials'. It would greatly reduce, said Newnham, the risk of broken limbs. It would greatly increase, said I, the risk of dying from exposure. But we went ahead, as we usually did when Newnham had one of his ideas.

I was mindful of my last drop into water, when I had almost drowned off the beach at Greystones in 1937. So when I popped out of the Whitley hole close behind Newnham and as soon as my chute had opened, I was off, steering like mad towards that tiny rowing-boat waiting on the Mere to pick us up. However, the crew of the boat knew where their priorities lay. Just as I had them in my sights, they started rowing off towards the point where Newnham was about to splash down.

One advantage of the X type was that the harness incorporated the Irvin 'quick release box', which required no more than a twist and a punch to release the chest and leg straps, so that when you hit the water you could slip straight out of the harness. It didn't make the water any warmer, though! It was icy! I had to wait while they hauled Newham into the boat, then we sat there shivering while the Whitley made another run to drop Captain Wooler, who was involved in training agents. He was wearing a rubber suit. Ironically, although it kept him warm, it also nearly killed him, for when he released the straps, instead of staying in the harness he slipped straight out of it and hurtled in from some fifty feet. The impact knocked him out, but his Mae West kept him afloat until we could drag him from the water. He spent a few weeks in hospital, and I let it be known that, if Newnham suggested any more water jumps for December, I would fill his Mae West with sand.

I never had any really dodgy jumps myself while I was at Ringway. Jumping from the balloon was a doddle, of course, and from the Whitley – providing you dropped nice and smoothly through the hole – there was little likelihood of anything going wrong with the chute. Chaps were still getting killed (there was quite a spate of them early in 1942) but that was usually because they botched their exits and either became tangled in their chutes or put high twists into the lines. The only time I came close to a messy end was not in a parachute but in a glider ...

Could we drop troops from gliders, somebody wanted to know. Only one way to find out. At that time, the only gliders we had at Ringway were eight-seat Hotspurs, built in furniture factories. I fitted X types to a couple of 200-pound dummies, and with Bob Fender at the controls, we were towed aloft by a Hawker Hind. While we were still climbing, I thought I might as well get the small side-door open. I should have studied that door more carefully. It was well forward in the tiny cabin, and as I released the catches, it was whipped out of my hands to lodge against the leading edge of the wing, where it acted as an off-centre and unwelcome air-brake. Bob Fender immediately cast off the tow. He had only partial control of the glider, and certainly not enough to avoid one of the tallest trees in the vicinity. When the noise of splintering woodwork died down, I was lying in a plywood junk-heap with a 200-pound dummy across my chest. Neither Bob Fender nor I had a scratch on us. Our lucky day, that was.

A more successful trial was one that we carried out at Henlow. Major Edwards, who organized the parachute training of our 'specials' from a mansion near Altrincham, had a very special 'special'. Apparently he was a French lawyer, who had to be delivered intact to a destination in France, yet who was so valuable that he could not be subjected to the risks of normal parachute training. We needed a parachute that would let him down gently and without oscillation. The parachute technicians at Henlow came up with the answer. They sewed three twenty-four-foot canopies together in a clover-leaf pattern, attached them to a single pair of liftwebs and devised a special pack to operate on the normal static-line system. I went down to Henlow for the trials, and the outfit certainly provided a stable ride at a gentle sixteen-feet per second rate of descent. Our 'special' was to take a radio transmitter with him, and we devised a system for packing it in sorbo and attaching it to the liftwebs so that it would not interfere with parachute deployment or land on the agent's head. I took the parachute back to Major Edwards, and I later heard that both the Frenchman and his radio had been delivered unharmed.

It was only a one-off piece of kit, for I think that, under intensive use, its opening characteristics might have been a bit dodgy. Once you start complicating a parachute, you are asking for long-term trouble. However, like many a war-time innovation, the triple-canopy chute was 'invented' much later as the 'trefoil' parachute, designed to provide means of assured opening for low-level delivery of paratroops.

I also did the first live drop from the Hudson. It was a far more comfortable aircraft than the Whitley. It had a roomier fuselage, and you could actually see what you were doing, but again there was no side door, and the exit had to be through a hole in the floor. In this case, however, there was room to attach a 'slide', which would help the parachutist to maintain a better body position as he shot into the airflow. At least, that was the theory: I was the one to test it.

I was wearing my best uniform and service cap when I turned up for the jump.

'You're not jumping like that, are you?' queried one of those who had come to watch. I assured him that I was. 'I bet you won't keep your hat on!'

'I bet I will,' I said.

I did, too. Jammed it on real tight, went down that slide and through the hole like a kid going into a swimming-pool, had a smooth opening and landed on my feet right in front of Newnham's office – still wearing my hat.

Nice aircraft, the Hudson, but there weren't enough of them available for parachuting, so they were used mainly for dropping 'specials' and small parties of troops. So it was that for the second major operation by Britain's young airborne force, Whitleys were again used ...

It was just over a year after X Troop had disappeared into Italy that our Ringway pupils went into action again, this time with more success: 119 paratroops under Major John Frost dropped at night onto the French coast north of Le Havre. Before taking off from Thruxton, they had passed the time consuming pints of tea, and the first thing most of them did when they landed in the darkness was to have a pee. Then they set about the Germans who were manning the Bruneval radar station. While the troops held off the defenders, Flight-Sergeant Cox of the RAF examined and dismantled the radar equipment and carted off its main components. The whole force then made a fighting withdrawal to the beach, from which they were lifted back to Portsmouth by Royal Navy landing-craft and destroyer. It was one of the most successful *coup-de-main* operations of the war and gave a great boost to the morale of British airborne forces – and their instructors.

At Ringway, the 'muscle mechanics' had been quick to learn the trade and soon had the place running the way Newnham wanted it. The training course was still confined to two weeks – not because Newnham had been persuaded by Bill Hire and me but because the Army was reluctant to devote more time to it. However, into that two weeks were now fitted J.C.K.'s ground-training programme and seven jumps, the first two from a balloon. I still thought that it was too many, and often said so. I thought they were making parachuting more complicated than it ever was, seeing more difficulties in it than ever existed. We had our own medical officer, who started to plot the incidence and nature of injuries, and they even turned the head-shrinkers loose on us. They wanted to investigate 'the terrors and phobias' involved in this 'inherently unnatural act' of leaping from aeroplanes. What a load of rubbish!

The story is told of one such boffin who was keen to examine the effects of a 'refusal' on the rest of the troops. He got the idea of joining a stick himself, 'refusing' to jump at a critical moment, then assessing the impact of this on the others. As he was a portly little gentleman, it was suggested that he might like to undergo some preparatory ground training. He insisted that this would not be necessary as he had no intention of actually jumping – merely 'refusing'. So the time came at 600 feet above Tatton Park when, incognito at the head of a stick and on the flash of the green light, our little head-shrinker braced himself at the aperture and cried loudly, 'I refuse to jump! I refuse to jump!'

'Like bloody 'ell you do!' muttered the PJI despatcher, and hurled the protesting figure bodily from the aircraft.

J.C.K. and I didn't always see eye to eye. I disagreed with some of his methods, and he certainly disagreed with some of mine. I suppose we represented the two extremes. He was a fine teacher and a bloody awful parachutist. I was a good parachutist and a bloody awful teacher. Actually, I think our combined talents were a fair mix, but Newnham didn't. Early in 1942 we trained several officers from the Physical Fitness Branch to take their place on the staff. 'Muscle mechanics with brains,' said Bill Hire. Our days at Ringway were coming to an end. It wasn't just that we were a professional embarrassment to Newnham: Bill Hire and I were also becoming socially unacceptable to him ...

Although we were never Newnham's favourite officers, he usually had us along whenever he entertained senior officers and local industrialists at his house in Wilmslow. He knew we could talk parachuting and would impress his guests with our stories, if not our manners. Most of those guests assumed that their vivacious hostess was Newnham's wife, but in fact she was still Miss Anne Finch-Hatton, sister of Dennis Finch-Hatton, the celebrated white hunter who had killed himself in an air crash in East Africa. Anne was quite a girl, and perhaps a little too partial to Bill and me. In the spring of 1942 she invited us to her thirtieth birthday party. We both danced with her and had a laugh or two. Later Newnham took us aside. He chatted for a while about the school and the new young officer instructors we had just trained and the way Airborne Forces were growing so rapidly, then said, 'You know ... I think your particular talents could be better used elsewhere.'

When he left us, Bill said, 'Harry, that bastard wants to get rid of us. We're cramping his style ...'

Within a month I was on my way. J.C.K. was promoted to squadron-leader to take a newly created post of chief instructor, and Newnham told me that my 'particular talents' would be best employed in Iraq, setting up a new parachute school.

Iraq? Not bloody likely. I was on the next train to London and was soon knocking on Leslie Hollinghurst's door in the Air Ministry. He arranged to have my posting to Iraq cancelled and for me to be appointed Air Liaison Officer to General 'Boy' Browning, overall commander of Britain's Airborne Forces, based at Netheravon. It caused a bit of a stink. Several senior officers told me how wrong I had been to go over Newnham's head like that. They didn't worry me. They might have been senior, but they weren't as senior as Hollinghurst.

It was ironic that, while he was gently giving me the boot from Ringway, Newnham was also recommending me for the Air Force Cross, which I received from King George later that year.

Shortly after my arrival at Netheravon, who should turn up there but Bill Hire! He had been posted from Ringway to set up a Parachute Maintenance and Support Unit. The Parachute Training School had now passed from the hands of the circus pros into those of the muscle mechanics.

They were to make a fine job of it, and continue to do so

today as we prepare to celebrate the fiftieth anniversary of the Parachute Training School at its modern home at RAF Brize Norton. I still think they over-train the brown jobs, though ...

14

With the 1st Airborne Division

Major-General 'Boy' Browning had been appointed to the overall command of Britain's Airborne Forces by Winston Churchill in person. The fact that they had briefly shared a dug-out on the Western Front during the First World War may have had something to do with it, but whatever the reason, it was a shrewd choice. Browning believed in massive airborne assault rather than small-party operations, and his persuasive enthusiasm and his influence in high places were to create two airborne divisions at a time when some – particularly in the senior ranks of the RAF – thought that one was too many.

As befits a Grenadier Guardsman, Browning was always immaculately turned out and was ever the perfect gentleman. I remember a do in the mess at Bulford, when amongst the group gathered around Browning and his wife, the novelist Daphne du Maurier, was a WAAF officer. When she wasn't looking, Bill Hire slipped an unwrapped 'French letter' into the top of her handbag. Sure enough, when the WAAF opened it to take out a handkerchief, onto the floor for all to see flopped this big pink condom. 'Boy' Browning was the only one who pretended not to notice.

I was on Browning's staff for only a short while before being moved to Bulford to join the 1st Airborne Division as an Air Liaison Officer – not, as might have been expected, to look after their parachuting affairs but to work with the glider boys of the 1st Airlanding Brigade. Gliders? From my Ringway experience in Bob Fender's Hotspur, the only thing I knew about gliders was how easily they could be converted into matchwood. Fortunately, I wouldn't have to spend much time in the things myself: my job would be to act for the brigade in its dealings with the RAF planning staffs and with the crews who would tow its gliders into battle. Many of them I already knew, from Ringway.

I was in good company at Bulford. I shared an office with the brigade major, Bill Howard, and I enjoyed living with the brown jobs. They had the right attitude. The brigade was commanded by 'Pip' Hicks, in whose office was a map of the Salisbury district, covering most of one wall and studded with red flags that obviously denoted something of great military importance. I ventured to ask what the flags represented.

'Pubs!' said the brigadier.

The 1st Airborne Division to which we belonged was commanded by Major-General 'Hoppy' Hopkinson. He was a right 'gung-ho' type! At Ringway he had seriously injured his back on his first parachute jump but had insisted on continuing his training by making water descents into Poole Harbour, still wearing his plaster cast. A man after my own heart.

There were certain advantages in being attached to the Army, the main one being the constant attention of my own batman, Fitzgerald. I was, however, rather conspicuous. When the division was visited by King George, mine was the only blue uniform amongst a sea of khaki.

'What's this?' asked the King, pointing his swagger-stick at me.

'Our mascot, sir,' said 'Hoppy'.

On the same occasion, King George visited No. 38 Wing at Netheravon, where he was taken by the Commander-in-Chief to see Bill Hire's Parachute Section.

'How many jumps have you done?' Air-Marshal Barratt asked Bill.

'Almost 600, sir.'

'No, no! How many have *you* done – personally?'

'About 600, sir,' repeated Bill.

'Six hundred parachute jumps!' said the King, 'And nothing to show for it!'

No medal ever came Bill's way.

Parachuting required a bit of nerve. Travelling in a glider, I thought, required even more. Being shot at, I decided after taking part in live-ammunition exercises, was the dodgiest business of all. At least, that was what I believed until I went to sea in a destroyer. I was given an opportunity in January 1943, to join HMS *Vivienne* on convoy escort duties in the North Sea. A pleasant cruise up the east coast, I thought. I boarded the vessel off Southend and was greeted by the captain, Lieutenant-Commander Leonard.

'You can bunk down in my day-cabin,' he said. 'I shan't be needing it during this run. I won't be leaving the bridge.'

'Why is that?' I asked.

'Torpedoes,' he said, cheerily. 'E-boats ... could put one in us any time.'

It wasn't the E-boats that bothered me: it was the weather. It was foul. The destroyer seemed to have a corkscrew motion all of its own, interrupted by sudden lurches as though it actually had been struck by a torpedo. I was sick as a dog.

'You'd be better up on deck, sir!' said a happy steward as I lay groaning in the captain's day-bunk.

So I staggered onto the deck, and as soon as I set foot on it, a wave like a hillside came over the rail and knocked me flying. I crawled back to the cabin and stayed there until the *Vivienne* was gliding down the Firth of Forth, heading for Rosyth.

'Are you coming back with us?' asked one of the officers.

'No bloody fear!' I told him, and caught the night train from Edinburgh. Put me in a Whitley with a parachute on. Even strap me into the seat of a glider. But never again put me on a destroyer in the North Sea.

Shortly afterwards, however, I did go to sea again, when the Airlanding Brigade moved out to North Africa. The 1st and 2nd Parachute Battalions were already there. They had jumped into action in November 1942 as part of the Allied invasion of North Africa. As paratroopers they had been misemployed in some poorly planned operations and had then fought in a pure infantry role, earning themselves the name 'The Red Devils' through a number of truly heroic actions. As the Germans and Italians were routed out of North Africa, it became the obvious launching-base for the invasion of southern Europe, called 'the soft underbelly of the Axis' by those who weren't actually going to do the fighting. The rest of the 1st Airborne Division was to move to Algeria to prepare for that invasion.

One of those advantages of being the sole RAF officer in an Army brigade was that, when I needed to, I could look after myself, so that when we embarked on the *Sterling Castle* at Liverpool docks, I was able to slip on board and bag one of the best cabins while the brown types were still sorting themselves out.

'Trust you blue jobs to get in first,' said 'Pip' Hicks, when he finally came on board to find me comfortably established.

It was an uneventful trip. We spent much of it playing poker and losing heavily to the RC padre, Father O'Houlighan. He had either divine assistance or cards up his sleeve.

We landed at Oran and were convoyed to Froha, an air-strip cut into a plain of red dust that was to be our training ground for the forthcoming action. It was to be a combined operation, involving the US 7th Army and Montgomery's 8th Army, each supported by its respective airborne division. The main airlift for the paratroops and the glider-borne force would come from the Americans, and there lay our problem. It was one that would lead us close to total disaster. The American crews had little or no experience of operational flying, and our glider pilots and small number of tug-crews were completely inexperienced in flying and towing the American Waco gliders that would form the major part of the Airlanding Brigade's transport. As the details of the operation were gradually revealed, the prospects became more daunting and the probability of a shambles more likely.

The plan to invade Sicily was centred on landings by the American 7th and British 8th Armies on targeted beaches on the southern and eastern coasts. Protection of the American beaches would be provided by paratroopers of the US 82nd Airborne Division, while the inland advance of the 8th Army would be eased by the capture of the Ponte Grande bridge by the 1st Airlanding Brigade and of the Primasole Bridge by the 1st Parachute Brigade. It was a good enough idea, and the troops were well capable of carrying it out – if they could be delivered to the target area. That was the snag: getting them there. The landings were to be at night, something never before attempted on a large scale even by experienced crews. There would be a long approach flight over the Mediterranean, a complex release pattern for the gliders, and no 'pathfinders' to mark the landing- and dropping-zones. It was a plan well beyond the capabilities of the crews expected to carry it out. Several of the more experienced operators realized this, and some of them said so. But 'Hoppy' himself, all heart and little actual experience of airborne operations, had personally approved the plan and had sold it to Montgomery without even consulting Browning. When Lieutenant-Colonel George Chatterton, commanding the British glider pilots, voiced his concern, 'Hoppy' told him either to relinquish his command or to get on with it. He got on with it. So did the rest of us.

The Americans were very much in the driving-seat as far as the detailed planning of the airlift was concerned. Sadly, Nigel Norman, who as an air commodore would have been our senior representative on the joint planning staff, never reached North Africa. He died when the Hudson that was bringing him out crashed on take-off from Portreath, in Cornwall.

While we waited for the Waco gliders to be taken from their crates and assembled at Froha, the paratroops began their practice. They had less of a problem and now had the luxury of at last jumping through the door of the DC-3 – which, as the 'Dakota', was now coming into general use for parachuting. In practical terms I would rather have been involved in their side of the operation, but by that time I had become firmly attached to the gliding boys. They were a grand bunch, and it was an honour to serve with them. At our level, we also got on well enough with the Americans. They were well provided with just about everything, except, strangely, liquor. They would give anything for a case of whisky. I exchanged some for a jeep, and enough cases of canned pineapple, fruit juice and candy bars to see the war out.

'Hoppy' had his headquarters in Mascara, in what had once been the bank. Mascara might once have been a pleasant French colonial town but was now full of troops to whom it offered little amusement other than an evil local wine and a range of 'liqueurs' which all tasted of bananas and industrial alcohol. Our main entertainment was provided by a half-witted Arab youth who thought he was a motor car. With sound-effects of amazing realism – including slamming doors, gear changes, dodgy brakes – he drove round and round the main square. It made his day when someone gave him a real steering-wheel.

When at last our glider pilots had some Wacos to play with, they found it pleasant enough to fly but were worried that, with its flat glide and lack of airbrakes, it didn't have the short-landing capability of our own Horsa. Nor, in the event of an over-high approach, could it be side-slipped with safety. Putting it down on the plain at Froha was all right, but landing it in Sicily, at night, would be a different kettle of fish. When there were enough gliders, we mounted a couple of mass-landing practices in daylight, but the largest night trial involved only twelve gliders. It was hardly realistic practice for what lay ahead, and by the time the training phase was over, our glider pilots had averaged a mere 4½ hours of flying in the Waco, including only slightly more than one hour at night. There had been no practice of a mass release in the dark, and very little landing training under simulated combat conditions. The American pilots of the 51st US Troop Carrier Wing who were to tow the gliders into battle had added little to their own experience. What was so obviously needed was for a bunch of the paratroops to go in before the gliders and mark the landing-strips and set up radio beacons to bring the 'tugs' in, but 'Hoppy' wouldn't hear of it.

A welcome addition to our force was the arrival in ones and twos of twenty-two Horsa gliders. They were the survivors of thirty-one that had left Portreath to be towed non-stop to North Africa by Halifaxes of 295 Squadron – a tremendous feat. I made one of those trips myself after a brief return to Britain, and it wasn't something that I wanted to repeat.

Towards the end of June, the division and its supporting gliders and aircraft moved to the mounting bases in Tunisia, close to the holy city of Kairouan. For the gliders and tugs, this meant a hairy flight over barren, 7,000-foot mountains. I chose to go by road.

My first job, for I was president of the mess committee, was to set up an officers' mess in our tented headquarters in an olive grove. I sent my batman, Fitzgerald, off to Sousse to see what he could find and, to prevent him from being shot for looting, gave him a signed authorization to 'remove articles' from hotels and other buildings. He returned with furniture, marble slabs and a bath – whose removal had caused some concern and a considerable flood in one of the town's hotels. I arranged for the mess to be provisioned by a French-Algerian Jew. Neither he nor I understood a word the other said, which is probably why we got on so well. Equipping and running that mess was one of my major contributions to the war effort!

The pressure was on, as everyone strove to prepare an inadequately trained force for the forthcoming operation. Those who had misgivings hid their feelings from the troops and the crews who were going to have to do the flying and the fighting, and 'Hoppy' himself remained supremely confident of the outcome. We all hoped he was right, but doubted it.

A few days before the airborne assault was launched, I went with Father O'Houlighan to a nearby convent. While he sat under a fig tree with the Mother Superior and a bottle of wine, I chatted to a pretty young Irish nun, the only one there who spoke English. Later I delivered a number of supply-parachutes of various colours and duly received three pairs of pyjamas made of multi-coloured nylon. By that time, Father O'Houlighan was not there to see them.

He was dead, in Sicily.

The delivery of the airborne forces to Sicily was the shambles that so many had forecast. On the evening of 9 July 1943, 143 gliders were towed into the air by 109 American-crewed Dakotas and thirty-four assorted Albermarles and Halifaxes of the RAF. Only sixteen of the gliders landed where they were supposed to land. Others were scattered all over eastern Sicily, and sixty-eight were released so far from the coast that they were forced to land in the sea. Over 500 men were drowned. 'Hoppy' had the folly of his optimism brought home to him when his own glider landed in the Mediterranean several miles from the coast of Sicily. He was picked up by a Royal Navy destroyer the following morning, and his humour was only slightly improved when he found that its captain had rowed with him in the same boat at Cambridge. 'Pip' Hicks, in a glider piloted by Chatterton himself, also landed in the sea but was close enough to swim ashore.

The small force that *was* delivered to the target took the Ponte Grande bridge and held it for eighteen hours before being overwhelmed. It was in that action that Father O'Houlighan was killed by a grenade.

The American paratroopers who jumped that night fared no better. Only 200 out of more than 3,000 landed in the target area on Gila Ridge. Some were dropped as much as sixty miles away. When the 'Red Devils' of the 1st Parachute Brigade went in on the night of 13 July, only a third of them were dropped within half-a-mile of the dropping zones. Twenty-nine of the 116 American planes didn't drop at all. It was on this occasion that the celebrated Alistair Pearson, commanding the 1st Battalion, drew his pistol and threatened to blow the American pilot's head off if he didn't fly through the flack barrier that our own and enemy guns were throwing up. Yet once more, the depleted force of airborne troops took – and in this case held – the Primasole Bridge.

But what a cock-up! Montgomery blamed the weather. Browning, more accurately, blamed the lack of training of the American air-crews. So, in retrospect, did 'Hoppy'. Nobody, at the time, blamed the brass who had conceived and approved a plan that was a recipe for disaster. What was quite certain was that no one could blame the troops, who fought magnificently – no matter where they landed. In fact, it was their guts and fighting ability that retrieved the situation, and the realities of the airborne delivery were hidden by the eventual success of the invasion, and the capture of Sicily.

It was some time before we ourselves had a fair picture of what had happened, although it was obvious from the reports of the returning air-crews that some of our worst fears had been realized. The greatest irony came a few days after the Airlanding Brigade had gone in. Lawrence Wright, as our senior ops officer at HQ, and some of the squadron-commanders and RAF staff were summoned to appear at the headquarters of the American Troop Carrier Wing. There, they stood at the back of a marquee behind a parade of the air-crews who had just scattered 5,000 men all over Sicily and its surrounding seas, to listen to a message from Eisenhower congratulating the American fliers on their magnificent achievement, to hear the announcement of immediate field promotions and to watch a medal being pinned on the chest of every American there.

Our gloom was lifted somewhat by a visit from 'Popski' and some of his 'private army', a bunch of absolute brigands who, like David Sterling's Special Air Service lads, roamed deep into the deserts of North Africa to hit the enemy where and when they least expected it. We marked their visit with a tremendous party out at 'Goubrine One', the airstrip for 296 Squadron, commanded by my friend from Ringway, Mac Monnies. The toilet facilities at the strip included a splendid six-seat 'thunder-box' of which the squadron was very proud and to which there was always a concerted rush first thing in the morning. The morning after Popski's visit, when the first customer raised one of the fly-trap lids, there was an almighty explosion that hurled the thunder-boxes and their contents over much of the camp. No wonder we won the war, with types like 'Popski' on our side.

When Sicily had been taken, the 1st Airborne Division

was committed to the Italian campaign as infantry. After they had taken Taranto, 'Hoppy', as thrustful as ever, was up with the forward troops when he was killed at Castanellata.

As the 1st Airlanding Brigade was no longer operating in an airborne role, it didn't need an Air Liaison Officer. After treating myself to a holiday on the coast at Hammamet, I asked for and was granted permission to return to Britain – if I could get there. I travelled by road to Algiers, then came to a halt at the end of a long waiting-list of people trying to get passages home. I could have been stuck there for months, but I managed to get a letter back to Hollinghurst, who was now commanding the newly formed 38 Group at Netheravon, and two weeks later I was switched to the head of the queue and put on a Dutch ship heading for Britain.

After a brief leave, I reported for duty at Netheravon as part of Hollinghurst's staff. It was like a Ringway reunion. Bill Hire was still there, running the parachute section; Mac Monnies was back with 296 Squadron; Bob Fender was experimenting with Horsa gliders; and Lawrence Wright soon returned from North Africa to share my office.

One of my first 'duties', with Bill Hire, was to attend Maurice Newnham's wedding in December 1943. He had decided to make an honest woman of Anne at last. He didn't invite us: she did, and we were the only PJIs there. We enjoyed a slap-up reception at the Savoy Hotel and still had time to take in the Windmill Theatre – and slip back-stage after the show.

Shortly after that, Bill suffered a sad fate. During a particularly busy period he had refused to grant leave to one of his WAAF packers, who in a fit of pique had complained to the 'Queen Bee' at Netheravon that Bill had made advances to her. No formal action was taken, but Bill Hire was on his way. The great irony was that, for once in his life, Bill hadn't even approached the girl!

I took over his duties, and if ever I had cause to have a WAAF come into my office, I made sure that I wasn't alone with her. Actually, they were a damn good bunch.

Their standard of packing was consistently high, and they were tremendous workers. When the Yanks were surprised and trapped at Bastogne during 'the Battle of the Bulge' in December 1944, I called all the girls in and had them working day and night right through the Christmas period, packing the chutes that were used to resupply the troops. We also dropped Alsatian dogs on that operation, and we had to have them muzzled so they didn't bite the girls when they were strapping the chutes to them. I recommended some of those kids for awards, but they never got them. The only people who really appreciated the worth of those girls were the troops who used the chutes they packed.

I spent the rest of the war at Netheravon, doing my little bit for the mounting of those great airborne assaults on Normandy, at Arnhem and across the Rhine. I watched with interest and some pride the growth of Britains airborne force into two full divisions – from those little seeds planted at Ringway in 1940 by Louis Strange and John Rock and a bunch of RAF fabric workers, Army PTIs and former circus jumpers.

At Netheravon I met Lord Trenchard for the first time. The great 'Father of the Royal Air Force', who had led it into independence in 1918 and had then retained that independence against stiff opposition during the 1920s, was an old man in 1944. We were watching Bob Fender diving a Horsa and demonstrating its brake-parachute when I noticed Trenchard wandering around, looking lost. He was wearing a uniform of ancient style, with turn-ups to the trousers. Nobody else recognized him. Not surprising: they hadn't been around when we had. I went to him and saluted.

'You'd get a better view from the control tower, sir,' I suggested.

He seemed pleased to be spoken to. 'Thank you, Squadron-Leader,' he said.

I felt like telling him what we 'erks' had thought of the 'MacDonald Bed' that he had introducd to the service in 1922. Instead of springs it had iron slats on which were placed three straw-packed 'biscuits'. It was agony. But I didn't remind him of those long-ago days. There was a war still going on.

In 1945, when it was over, my own career in the RAF came to an end. I would like to have stayed, but I had upset a few people along the line and could imagine what some of them would have written on my confidential reports. 'Ward is an outspoken fellow, with a mind of his own ... shows little respect for authority,' Newnham and some of the others would have said. That's right. Bruce Williams, Bill Hire and I – that was how we were. The peace-time Air Force, I realized, would have little room for the likes of us. I might have gone to 'Holly' had he still been along the corridor, but by then he had been transferred to duties in the Far East. So I left.

In a way, it was fitting to leave the service from Netheravon. It was there, almost twenty years earlier, that I had landed after my first cross-country flight with Leslie Hollinghurst. It was there that I had made my first free-fall parachute jump from the old Vimy when I joined 'The Loonies' in 1927.

It was a place of good memories.

15

Since Then ...

My involvement with the services wasn't completely severed, for through an acquaintance I managed to get a job with NAAFI, the armed forces' own club-and-canteen service. I had asked to serve overseas and was sent to Naples, then to Rome. I did the rounds and saw the sights in both cities and was then told to report to Athens, where there might be a job for me to do. There wasn't. I again did the town, this time in the company of an old friend from the Airlanding Brigade, and was then sent by Liberty Ship to Salonika, where at last a job awaited me. I was to establish an officers' club.

We hired a large house from a Greek tobacco merchant who was very charming and hospitable, just as he had been to the Germans when they had been in occupation. I furnished the place, fitted it out in style, turned the front garden into an open-air restaurant with bar and sunken dance-floor, hung the trees with coloured lights and contracted an excellent staff. I say it myself, but it was a good club.

There were, of course, rival establishments in Salonika which offered certain amenities that I was not in a position to provide. The Mediterranean had a popular upstairs bar, presided over by 'Mimi', who – in addition to other accomplishments – was a fine darts-player. Probably the most notorious hostess was 'Biting Mary' of the Argentina Night Club. It was often quite obvious on the beach in the morning which officer(s) had been entertained by Biting Mary during the previous night. One of her customers was our C of E padre. He also used to lead off our regular Friday evening parties with a rendition of 'The Ball of Kirremuir'.

While I was at Salonika, Major-General 'Eric' Down took over as General Officer Commanding British Troops in Greece – old 'Dracula' of Ringway days. He invited me to dinner at his villa on the slopes above the town and said, 'We can't have you living down there in the club: we must get you a place up here.'

An officer in 'Claims and Hirings' was instructed to prepare a villa for me, and the engineers put in a field telephone to connect me with the club. The great thing about airborne types is that they look after each other! When Down moved his headquarters to Athens, he insisted that I go there too, to take over the officers' club in the city.

It was a good life in Greece – cheap living, and not without its excitements. However, I overstayed my welcome. I was on a two-year contract in Athens and had over-run by a few weeks when I was summoned to the Embassy and had my passport taken away. A few days later, the police came to the club, took me to the docks and under heavy escort put me on board the SS *Sumaria*, Britain-bound. I was being deported! The other passengers were convinced that I was an international crook.

That was 1948. I took one look at post-war, rationed Britain and asked to be sent overseas again. I was given a job as manager of a club for the Control Commission in Germany – the Lakeside Club at Ramscheide. It was idyllic, built beside a lake in forested country where deer and wild boar ran free. It was a good spot to fall in love, which I did with a beautiful German blonde, called Erica, who became my wife.

After Ramscheide, there was the Linden Club outside Cologne, where I met Maurice Newnham and Anne, who were living in Düsseldorf at that time. Then, in 1950, Erica and I came back to Britain, and Yorkshire.

For twenty years I ran a succession of pubs and hotels. The first was the Black Horse in Otley. 'Eric' Down wrote me a recommendation for the job, and the interviewer on behalf of the company just happened to be ex-Major Hargreaves who had been on the Ringway staff in 1940. I got the job ... Then there was the Bellevue in Bradford, close to the football ground; the Reservoir, also in Bradford; and lastly the Causeway Foot Inn on the edge of the moors near Halifax.

Familiar faces kept turning up. Sometimes a reporter would appear and write an article in one of the Yorkshire or national papers about 'The Yorkshire Birdman', and that would prompt a few old friends to call in – Jimmy King from air circus days, PJIs from Ringway, airborne types from X Troop and the Airlanding Brigade.

One day somebody I didn't recognize slapped a photo on the bar and said, 'Remember that?'

I certainly did. It was *The Spider* in India, with a coach-and-four drawn up alongside it. The chap had been one of the Army officers who had welcomed Andrews and Ginger and me when we made that unscheduled landing at Sargodha.

When I finally retired to our house at Knaresborough, Erica thought I should take up art again, to keep myself occupied, so I enrolled at the Harrogate Art School. The tutor was a man after my own heart. He favoured landscape painting. We would go out into the countryside, and when he found a likely spot, he would set the others to work while he and I retired to the nearest inn. I got to know every pub within ten miles to the north and west of Harrogate and never made a sketch.

I was never tempted, after the war, to put on another parachute, nor to take those black wings out of the attic to which they had been consigned. The days of the flying circus and the professional jumper were well and truly over. Oh, there were a few air shows coming back in the 1950s, and one or two ex-PJIs and airborne types giving free-fall displays at them, but there was no living to be made from it. In France, a former member of the French Special Air Service who had trained at Ringway in 1943, Leo Valentin, made a name for himself as a free-faller when he rediscovered the skills of body control that Arthur East had known back in the twenties. Then Valentin added wings to his display jumping, as Clem Sohn and I had. He applied 'aerodynamic principles' to the construction of wings made of plywood, but 'aerodynamic principles' couldn't save him when he smashed a wing-tip against the door of the Dakota when he jumped at Speke in 1955, and he died as Clem Sohn had, under a tangle of chutes and wings. I could have told him about making exits on a plank to keep the wings out of trouble, and about quick-release devices ...

Nowadays, the young breed of skydivers are flying their bodies pretty well without wings, and their 'square' parachutes have capabilities we never dreamed of under our plain round canopies. I admire them tremendously, but I have no cause to envy them. I had my thrills. I had my fun. I had my day.

Mind you, I'm only eighty-seven, so haven't given up the air altogether. Both my sons became proficient glider pilots when they were young. One of them, young Harry, now gets his kicks from crewing on ocean racing yachts. The other, Malcolm, is a squadron-leader in the Royal Air Force. He has parachuted for fun and flies light aircraft as a hobby. I go up with him and take the controls whenever I get the chance. He is currently taking up a one-third ownership of a Stampe – an open-cockpit biplane, all wind and wires and smell of the engine. Just like the old days, that will be.

I can't wait to get my hands on it ...

Index